The fall of Constantinople was followed by four long centuries of stifling Ottoman rule through which the Greek race lived a precarious existence. The Orthodox Church struggled desperately to keep alive the national consciousness of the race and eventually succeeded in bringing about a renewed vigor and determination that was to lead to a free Greek nation many years later.

The seventeenth century marks a turning point in this long period of Ottoman rule. The author deals with this obscure period by building up his story around the central character Paisius Ligarides, one of the most learned clergymen of his time. His life spans the middle period of the four centuries of Turkish domination and his lifetime marks in many ways the turning point in the history of modern Greek literature. Most of his works are as yet unpublished and it is on the basis of these manuscripts that the author attempts to bring to life both the man and his times. This is the first full-length study of Paisius Ligarides to appear.

ABOUT THE AUTHOR

A Byzantinist, lexicographer, Greek scholar and war hero, Harry Hionides is widely travelled and now teaches at Athens College. He has degrees from Columbia and Oxford and has been a Junior Fellow of Dumbarton Oaks. Born in Canton, Ohio, of Greek parentage, he has published a wide range of books and articles including several dictionaries of which an English-Greek Technical Dictionary is a standard work. He has recently completed a translation of *Byzantium in the Seventh Century* and is editing *Byzantine Wall-Paintings of Crete* which will circulate shortly.

TWAYNE'S WORLD AUTHORS SERIES

A Survey of the World's Literature

GREECE

Paisius Ligarides

(*TWAS 240*)

TWAYNE'S WORLD AUTHORS SERIES (TWAS)

The purpose of TWAS is to survey the major writers —novelists, dramatists, historians, poets, philosophers, and critics—of the nations of the world. Among the national literatures covered are those of Australia, Canada, China, Eastern Europe, France, Germany, Greece, India, Italy, Japan, Latin America, the Netherlands, New Zealand, Poland, Russia, Scandinavia, Spain, and the African nations, as well as Hebrew, Yiddish, and Latin Classical literatures. This survey is complemented by Twayne's United States Authors Series and English Authors Series.

The intent of each volume in these series is to present a critical-analytical study of the works of the writer; to include biographical and historical material that may be necessary for understanding, appreciation, and critical appraisal of the writer; and to present all material in clear, concise English—but not to vitiate the scholarly content of the work by doing so.

Paisius Ligarides

By HARRY T. HIONIDES
Athens College

Twayne Publishers, Inc. :: New York

Library of Congress Catalog Card Number: 70–187634

MANUFACTURED IN THE UNITED STATES OF AMERICA

To Bill Dipson

Preface

Scholars and historians, with few notable exceptions, have tended to ignore the Greek world of the seventeenth century; for most, interest in the eastern Mediterranean and the Balkan areas ceased with the capture of Constantinople in 1453. Attention was devoted for the most part to the remarkable events and developments that took place in western Europe.

Yet, this very neglected part of the world did not cease to play an increasingly important role in the centuries following the downfall of Constantinople, for developments there were destined eventually to culminate in the dissolution of the once mighty and invincible Ottoman Empire and in the birth and growth of new national consciousnesses that today dominate this vital crossroads of the world.

The Greek Orthodox church was the sole surviving force that nurtured the hopes of millions of subject Christians through four centuries of oppressive and stifling domination by the Turks. It must be admitted, however, that although the Ottomans brought Greece under a worse domination politically than did the Venetians and Genoese before them, they nevertheless assured the Greeks a greater religious liberty. The Ottoman government was theocratic in form, and in its eyes, religion and politics constituted an inseparable entity. The subject Christians consequently were recognized as an independent religious group and, hence, as a separate civil institution. Thus, we find the patriarch of Constantinople acting as both the civil and the religious head of his race. The Greeks were able as a result to survive as a distinctive unit throughout the four long centuries of Turkish rule.

But, to survive under the Ottomans, the Greek church paid a heavy price, and it declined rapidly from its former great estate. The outward restrictions which were imposed upon the church were not, however, as degenerative as was the inner decay resulting from the relationships with the Turkish government. Corruption and intrigue sapped the higher administration of the church. Each new patriarch, upon assuming the throne, traditionally made a gift to the sultan to confirm his spiritual and secular authority. It became the established practice to pay the sultan a large sum of money to obtain his official blessing; and naturally enough, it was in the interest of the sultans to change the patriarch as often as possible for greater gain. Hence, patriarchs were removed and reinstated at will. The noxious effects of bribery and intrigue among the higher clergy at Constantinople and other sees contributed further to the rapid decline of the church.

Added to this was the sad state of learning in the Greek world. Both the clergy and the laity were for the most part illiterate, and books were in short supply. Inevitably, the once pristine brightness of the faith as preached by the great fathers of the church was lost. It became more and more obscure and faded. Teaching from the pulpit, by which means the spiritual side of religion is normally maintained, was unhappily lacking. Though learning never wholly disappeared among the Greeks under Turkish rule, the conditions nevertheless in the seventeenth century were not conducive to learning. There were few theologians, and when a Greek scholar wished to pursue higher studies, he had no alternative but to resort to European universities. Most Greeks studied in Italy where the University of Padua was one of the more popular centers of learning. In many ways, Padua was the Oxford of modern Greece. Thus, Greek Orthodoxy suffered still further, for the seminarians were of necessity trained by either Catholic or Protestant teachers, so that they often returned to their parishes as "Romanizers" or "Protestantizers."

In this way the original faith of the Orthodox church became distorted. The Greek church relapsed into a state of passive resistance, struggling only to preserve the barest tenets of Christianity. The single bright facet in this dismal period of the history of the church was the devotional aspect of the Greek people. The adherence to, and preservation of, the outward forms of religion helped save the church from extinction. In the final analysis, it was the virtues of the rural population and not the power of the church that preserved the race. And the survival of the Greeks depended finally on the character and fortitude of the people themselves, which could only be partially strengthened by the influence of the clergy.

In times of despair, hope may be engendered and nurtured in the breast of man by books of prophecies, by astrological phenomena, by the occult sciences, and by other kinds of divination. The need for assistance in making decisions, the hope of finding explanations for the apparently inexplicable, and the necessity for interpretation of events, whether natural or political, were provided for by astrologers, dream interpreters, theologians, palm readers, and the like. To fulfill an existing need, the art of prognostication became an integral part of every religion. Consequently, prophetic literature abounded in the Middle Ages, and this literature enjoyed a vast popularity. In the sixteenth and seventeenth centuries, during which the occult sciences and witch trials were very much in vogue, there existed the highest flowering of star gazing, divination, and the prophetic arts, for it was a time of great uncertainty, and superstition drove men to a feverish quest for reassurance. Both in eastern and in western Europe prophecies had a wide circulation, the *Centuries* of Nostradamus being but one of many. Shakespeare, Donne, and Bacon dealt at considerable length with the occult sciences. In the words of King Lear, "It is the stars, the stars above us, govern our condition."

The Greek world also turned to the prophecies, but with even greater intensity, for reassurance and hope. Especially popular were the rhymed prognostications of which a confusing agglomeration has survived from the Byzantine period. Obscure and symbolic in many instances, these predictions could be interpreted in a way to suit the particular needs of the people at a particular time. In the vast corpus of prophetic books, many of which were circulated in manuscript form, two recurring themes stand out, and these were the things that the Greek people wanted to believe: after a certain period of years, the race of the Ottomans would be driven out of Constantinople and would be driven to the depths of Asia whence they came, whereupon a Greek emperor would once again reign supreme (or that a Constantine lost Constantinople and a Constantine would recover it); and a fair, or blond, race from the North or the East would liberate the Greeks from bondage. The Russians were understood to be the blond race until as late as the early part of the twentieth century.

And not surprisingly, during World War I, some propagated the belief that the liberating fair race from the North would be the German nation. In other words, circumstances and the political situation determined the interpretation of the prophetic words.

The widest-circulating book of prophecies was a much later collection under the pseudonym of Agathangelos. It was the work of a learned cleric of the eighteenth century, a copy of which could be found in most Greek homes. Its basic theme was that a certain eastern race (that is, the Russians) would come to the help of the Greeks, and joining forces with them would push the Turks back to Mecca. This particular oracle was deliberately cultivated and circulated by some of the emerging leaders of the Greek national movement in the period before the Greek War of Independence. Another prediction made by this visionary was that Constantinople would again become the capital of the Greeks. Agathangelos also foretold the fate of other European nations, including Austria, France, England, and Spain. This and similar books of prophecies served as useful tonics to raise the hopes of the despondent Greeks. And these books served their purpose well.

Paisius Ligarides stands astride the gloomy seventeenth century as an intellectual giant. Though his character leaves much to be desired, though he was an opportunist of the first order, and though he had the bad habit of twisting facts to suit his own ends, we nevertheless find depicted in his fascinating life and travels a representative type of cleric who was, unfortunately, altogether too common in the rather decadent moral milieu of the Greek world of the seventeenth century. It goes without saying that he nowhere rises to the intellectual and Christian heights of a Cyril Lukaris, the most distinguished Greek Orthodox prelate since Photius (though a "Protestantizer"), who met his tragic end in the hangman's noose at the time that Paisius was in Rome; nor of that other theologian and contemporary, Dositheus, patriarch of Jerusalem (who occasionally slipped into "Romanizing" ways), who defrocked Paisius when he was in Moscow some thirty years later. Nevertheless, Paisius Ligarides was one of the few cultivated and able theologians of the century. Since the Greek world of the seventeenth century remains relatively unknown, and since Paisius reflects more than any other the social, religious, and moral patterns of the period, a detailed description of his life and travels would not, I feel, be out of place in a book of this kind. In the character of Paisius we find mirrored the insecurity, the fear of the morrow, the lack of confidence, and the by-product of all these —opportunism, but at the same time the burning desire for a brighter future, which are all so typical of the seventeenth century—and which are so applicable to the century in which we now live.

HARRY THEODORE HIONIDES

Athens, Greece
1971

Acknowledgments

My first acquaintance with Paisius Ligarides and the unique manuscript of the *Book of Prophecies* began in the congenial and scholarly atmosphere of the Dumbarton Oaks Research Library some sixteen years ago.

Professors Cyril Mango and Basil Laourdas had then encouraged me to copy out and to examine at length the voluminous work, a microfilm copy of which existed in the Library of Congress.

Professor Mary P. Gianos kindly suggested that I write this book for Twayne's World Authors Series. It is the first study in depth of a more or less completely unknown and yet very significant Greek author of the seventeenth century. And for this opportunity I am indebted to her.

Contents

Chronology

1609–
1610 Paisius Ligarides born in Chios.

1623 Enters Saint Athanasius College in Rome. Leo Allatius returns Palatine Library to Rome.

1636 Submits doctoral thesis on philosophy and religion before assembly of cardinals. Begins teaching at Saint Athanasius.

1637 Edits *De Purgatorio igne adversus Barlaam* by his late teacher Petros Arcudius. Prefaces it with a flattering letter to Pope Urban VIII, two epigrams to the pontiff, and an elegy to Arcudius.

1638 Cyril Lukaris murdered in Constantinople. Paisius continues teaching in Rome.

1639 Ordained deacon and then priest of the Roman Catholic church.

1642 The Congregatio Propaganda Fidei sends him to the East to work for the union of the churches. Writes letters to Allatius from Zante, Chios, and Galata.

1643 Writes to Allatius from Constantinople asking for an increase in subsidy from Rome. Works secretly to proselytize the Greeks.

1647 Receives from the patriarch of Constantinople letters of recommendation as a bona fide Orthodox for his visit to the Danubian provinces.

1651 Meets the patriarch of Jerusalem and accompanies him to Palestine where he is tonsured as an Orthodox monk.

1652 Is consecrated Metropolitan of Gaza. Begins *History of the Greek Patriarchs of Jerusalem.*

1654 Passes through Chios and corresponds with Allatius.

1655 Teaches in Bucharest. Completes his monumental *Book of Prophecies.*

1656 Dedicates the *Book of Prophecies* to Czar Alexis of Russia and calls upon him to liberate the Greeks.

1657 Reluctantly allows two copies of his *Book of Prophecies* to be made by the monk Baba Yani for the visiting patriarch Macarius of Antioch. Is invited by Patriarch Nicon to come to Moscow to help edit and revise the liturgical books of the Russians. Continues to receive funds from Rome.
1660 Czar Alexis summons an irregular synod to depose Nicon.
1661 Allatius becomes director of the Vatican Library.
1662 Arrives in Moscow.
1663 Writes various letters to the patriarchs of Jerusalem and Constantinople.
1666 The trial of Nicon begins. Paisius presides over the synod, and Nicon is condemned.
1668 Dedicates his *History of the Condemnation of Nicon* to Czar Alexis. A letter arrives in Moscow from the patriarch of Jerusalem stating that his predecessor had defrocked Paisius when he had been in the Danubian provinces.
1669 The czar intercedes with the patriarch of Jerusalem on behalf of Paisius and asks that he be absolved.
1670 Letters of forgiveness are sent to Moscow by the new patriarch of Jerusalem. Negotiations are conducted between Paisius and Heinsius for the manuscript of *The Homilies of Photius.*
1671 Dositheus, patriarch of Jerusalem, defrocks Paisius.
1672 Royal decree issued ordering Paisius to leave Moscow and to return to Palestine to clear his position with Dositheus.
1673 Leaves Moscow for Kiev from where he refuses to budge. The grand dragoman of the Porte writes to the czar asking that Paisius not be allowed to leave Russia. In Moscow a Slavic version of the *Book of Prophecies* is dedicated to the czar by Spatharius.
1674 Ordered back to Moscow.
1675 Writes to the czar protesting against the attitudes of the political and ecclesiastical authorities of Kiev and against Dositheus.
1676 Receives permission to leave Russia. Czar Alexis dies.
1677 Goes to Kiev and remains there.
1678 Dies a broken and lonely man. Buried by order of the new czar in the Monastery of the Brotherhood of the Epiphany in Kiev.
1681 Nicon dies in exile.

CHAPTER 1

The Early Years

CHIOS, on the island of the same name, was, after Constantinople and Smyrna, the most prosperous and learned city in the expansive Ottoman Empire, but with a difference, for the latter two far more populous centers contained a large proportion of Turkish inhabitants, and Ottoman rule was everywhere evident. Many travelers of the seventeenth century remarked on the lack of Turkish influence in Chios where "a few turbans here and there" [1] were the only signs of their presence on the island.

The island owed its enviable prosperity to thriving commerce, to the special privileges granted it by the sultans, which in effect made of it a semiautonomous domain, and most of all to the character of the inhabitants themselves, whose preeminent moral temperament was acknowledged throughout the eastern Mediterranean. The ill-repute enjoyed by the Greek merchant class generally was widespread, and this reputation was one of rapacity, dishonesty, and insolence.[2] The inhabitants of Chios, on the other hand, were blessed with better educational facilities, a spirit of cooperation in the community devoid of envy and dissension and enhanced by strong family bonds. Idleness was frowned upon, and Chios was the only city of all Greek cities where there existed no class of idlers who preoccupied themselves with soliciting various positions from their Turkish masters as tax collectors or intriguing with the local pasha to obtain better posts in the church hierarchy, and other such sordid practices. The much superior morality of the islanders in all their dealings, whether among themselves or abroad and their reputation of unflagging honesty, helped make Chios the most prosperous and thriving area in the whole of the Greek-speaking world for several centuries.

I *Chios and Pride of Country*

It was in such blissful surroundings, or as the Greeks and foreign travelers both were wont to say, "in the world's most favored spot," that Paisius Ligarides was born in 1609 or 1610. His father John and mother Orietta Callaronis resided in the Catholic quarter of the city where the newborn was baptized Panteleimon or Pantoleon, the name he was to retain until tonsured as an Orthodox monk forty-one years later. Both parents were of the Catholic rite, having been converted like so many of their compatriots to the Roman faith. On the basis of reports and memoirs written by the numerous visitors of that century, it is estimated that the Orthodox population was three times as large as the Catholic in the city, whereas in the countryside the great majority of inhabitants practiced the Greek faith.[3]

The name of Ligarides had survived, at least until quite recently, in a small ruined church which was probably the family chapel. There are also on record a Paisius dating to the years before the Turkish conquest of the island, and a Demetrius and George of the seventeenth century.[4] It is very probable that this was an ancient Chiote family that had been proselytized by Catholic missionaries in the previous century. One scholar has referred erroneously to Pantoleon and Paisius as two different persons, the former being identified as Orthodox, and the latter as Catholic born, although they are both one and the same.[5]

Paisius was enrolled by his parents in a school run by Jesuits. This devoted and energetic Catholic order, founded by Saint Ignatius Loyola less than a hundred years before to fight the disruptive influences of the Protestant Reformation movement on the Continent, had spread its activities to eastern Europe and the Greek-speaking world, where it made systematic and concerted efforts to proselytize and bring into the Catholic fold the now weakened remnants of the once powerful and proud Orthodox family. Greece was overrun by monastic orders of the West and the papacy worked for the subjection of the Orthodox Greeks, no longer through persecution as in the earlier centuries, but through persuasion. And the Order of Jesus was among its ablest and most dedicated agents. A church torn by petty dissensions and led for the most part by uninspired and selfish ecclesiastics provided fertile ground for the dissemination of Catholic dogma.

Contemporary travelers have commented at length on the activities of the several Catholic orders that existed in Chios. The English visitor John Covel writes, "In these [convents] there are severall schooles (the Jesuites have three) where Greekes goe as well as others, and afterwards they are removed to Italy to study; therefore you may expect that ye Romane tenets must needs by degrees be propagated."[6] The year in which Paisius was born William Lithgow visited the island and gave an English gentleman's colorful version of these activities:

> At last I arrived at the Citty of Scio, where I was lodged, and kindly used with an old man, of the Genuesen race, for the space of eight dayes: I found here three Monasteries of the order of Rome, one of the Jesuits, another of Saint Francis, and the third of the Dominican Friers, being all come from Genua; and because the greatest part of the Citty is of that stocke, and of the Papall Sea, these Cloyesters have a braver life for good cheare, fat Wines, and delicate leachery, than any sort of Friers can elsewhere find in the world.[7]

In 1622 when Paisius was yet twelve years old, Pope Gregory XV had organized in Rome a committee of hierarchs to unify and supervise the work of foreign missions, and this committee was known as the Congregatio de Propaganda Fide (Congregation for the Propagation of the Faith).[8] It was through the efforts of this group that many Chiotes were sent for higher learning in Rome where they were exposed further to the Catholic dogma.

The orders worked openly and without hindrance in the island. Friction did exist between the Orthodox and Catholics, and among the former there was an underlying suspicion of Rome and the activities of its missionaries. Since the Catholic teachers were as a rule far more educated and better qualified than their Orthodox counterparts, the islanders would often revert to them for spiritual instruction. Despite the underlying suspicion and friction between the communities, it is surprising how good and harmonious were the relationships between the Greeks and the Roman Catholics, especially in Chios and the islands, at least during the sixteenth and in part of the seventeenth centuries. Common worship in the same church was often the practice, and intermarriage was not uncommon.

At the age of thirteen, Paisius made preparations to leave Chios for Rome, probably through the efforts of his lifelong friend and compatriot, the fanatical Catholic Leo Allatius. He was not to return to his birthplace until 1641, nearly two decades later. The long absence from Chios was to increase rather than diminish his nostalgic fondness for the island. Pride of birthplace was deeply ingrained in him, and this was a characteristic so universally Greek. Throughout his many years of travel and vicissitudes of fortune, he retained unimpaired affection for his native land and never missed an opportunity to sing its praises. Homer, of whom he became inordinately fond when he had completed his Roman education, was in his eyes without a doubt a Chiote, and he would go so far as to maintain that the great ancient poet Simonides was not from Keos but from Chios. Moreover, Byzantium's outstanding general Belisarius was not an Illyrian but a Chiote. The enthusiasm for his birthplace often carried him to extreme lengths of deliberately distorting historical facts that referred to the island; and we know that when he was in Rome, he actually wrote a history of Chios which has not survived, unless it exists in collections of manuscripts which have not yet been discovered. References to this history known as the *Chian Chiliads* are numerous in the *Book of Prophecies* wherein Paisius cites several passages.

II *Rome and the Formative Years*

Paisius left Chios in the late spring of 1623 and did not return to his birthplace for nearly twenty years. Arriving in Rome in June, he was enrolled in the Greek College the following month.

Saint Athanasius, the Greek College of Rome, had been founded by Pope Leo X more than one hundred years before for the education of young Greeks, but the school did not come into its own until much later when it was revived by Pope Gregory XIII in 1557 for the purpose of training Greeks, Ruthenians, Italians, and others who would eventually work as missionaries abroad for the union of the churches or the primacy of Rome. The Greeks never numbered more than a handful at any particular time and constituted always a small minority in the school. Some died in the college; others abandoned their studies for one reason or another. Students who were incapable of good training returned to their homes soon after entering. Others rejoined their families at the age of seventeen or eighteen on account of bad health before completing their schooling. Of those who graduated, a few remained in Italy for fear of going back to their homeland, while yet others risked the hostility of their countrymen by returning and preaching the blessings of what in their eyes was the true faith. A few who finished would return to their birthplace driven by love of country or family, and these would spread the Catholic teaching surreptitiously within the family circle and remain loyal to the Roman dogma. Yet, there was a handful of young Greeks trained at the college who, once having rejoined their friends and families, renounced the pope and returned into the fold of Orthodoxy. A few of the latter became outspoken critics of the Catholic church, at least on the surface, and Paisius Ligarides fell into this latter category.

Young Paisius began his studies with grammar, and the next year, while still fourteen, moved on to the humanities and rhetoric after which he spent three years in philosophy followed by four years of theology. He soon began to display his remarkable talents. An outstanding scholar in all respects, he made the best of his opportunities and in the opinion of many of his contemporaries was one of the most learned men of the seventeenth century. He became particularly adept in the art of rhetoric in which he distinguished himself for sharpness and readiness and for copious learning. His masterly elocution was to prove most useful to him in his many peregrinations in the East when with great facility he could support the Latin or the Greek position with equal ease and fluency. Few could withstand his force of argument when he proved the preeminence of the papal authority or when he supported the prerogatives of the patriarch of Constantinople. Speaking and writing both Latin and Greek, intimately acquainted with the theology and ritual of both churches, initially a Latin in belief and eventually a practicing Greek Orthodox, Paisius was well prepared to argue on either side and to conform to either communion when occasion demanded and personal gain and prestige were at stake.

The fickle pendulum of history again had made a full swing in a westerly direction. Italy became the repository of the vast corpus of ancient Greek learning. For the second time in the history of civilization, the arts and letters that have embellished the western way of life were scattered by the Greeks over the world in the wake of a national catastrophe, and for the second time the unfortunate race suffered denigration on the part of those very peoples who had reaped the rich rewards of this knowledge. The epithet

Greek became, and for long endured, as a synonym of all that was mean and treacherous. In western Europe at least, the Trojans had become the heroes while the Achaeans, of whom Odysseus was the representative type, were the wily rogues. From as early as the fifteenth century, Rome, Venice, and Padua, among other cities, became the great centers of Greek learning; and it was in these same centers that the Greeks were reintroduced to their rich past. From these cities knowledge of the classics was disseminated to the very areas from which they had originally sprung. Like all Greeks of his time, Paisius was very conscious of his direct ties with Byzantium, and it was not until he had studied in Rome that he became fully cognizant of the classical heritage of his race. The awareness and pride of this classical patrimony came very late to the Greeks, and when all is said and done, it was the westerners who redirected the Greeks from the path of their living Byzantine heritage onto the path of their nearly defunct classical legacy. Until this innovation from the West, the Greeks were intimately conscious of their Byzantine past and in their eyes the empire of Byzantium which had been overthrown by their Ottoman masters would be enslaved only temporarily and would one day be reconstituted. The Greeks looked longingly to Constantinople as their capital, and Athens did not become the final spiritual and intellectual head of the race until as late as 1922 when the curtain would come crashing down, finally and irrevocably, to end forever the grand national dream of recovering the historic "city of all cities," the fountainhead of orthodoxy.

Homer, Herodotus, Hesiod, and Hippocrates were names that rang familiarly in their ears and were vaguely and mistily recognized in their subconscious—but only as names. They were on more familiar grounds with the fathers of the church, and closer still were the numerous saints on whose stories the Greeks were nurtured daily. The Scriptures and the lives of the saints constituted the sources for most of their learning and lore, and this knowledge was tempered by the strong belief in miracles and prophecies which promised them eventual succor from their oppressive Moslem masters.

In the course of his long stay in Rome, Paisius was exposed to the intellectual excitement that had swept across the Continent. Classical authors, both Latin and Greek, were everywhere in demand. Hundreds of hitherto unpublished manuscripts saw the light of day at the famous presses of Europe and new editions were being printed in ever larger numbers. The works of most of the ancients had become accessible finally to a wider audience of readers. In the year that Paisius arrived in Rome, for instance, the first printed edition of the scandalous and controversial *Secret History* of Procopius appeared in Lyons. This had been edited by Alamannus, who had taught at the Greek College, and who had discovered the manuscript in the Vatican Library.

Paisius acquired a passionate fondness for books, and he never lost this bibliomania. Having ready access to the rich libraries of Rome, he took maximum advantage of these collections and being an avid reader became deeply versed in both the ecclesiastical writers and the classical authors. Nor did he neglect his Byzantine heritage, for he was to use much of the writings of Zosimus, Cedrenus, and Zonaras for his historical sources when compiling the voluminous *Book of Prophecies.* In a very curious and rare book, *The Travels of Macarius,* written by one Archdeacon Paul of Aleppo who had met Paisius in the Danubian provinces some fifteen years after he had abandoned Rome, the Archdeadon says:

> We were told by that eminently learned man, Kyr Paisius, the Sciot, that he had travelled into all the European countries, and resided in the great city of Rome for a length of time; that he went up to the Pope's Library, the number of religious and pious books in which amounts to 72,000 copies, each single, and this is a thing well known; that, among them all, he was unable to find a second copy of this book [*The Exposition of the Psalms*], which is therefore unique in the world.[9]

Paisius had a brilliant teacher, one Petros Arcudius, who had devoted a lifetime to propagating the Catholic faith in Poland and southwestern Russia. Arcudius, like Leo Allatius, though Greek, was a fanatical and devoted supporter of the Papacy, and had written many polemical tracts attacking the "schismatic Greeks." Pope Urban was very active in the program to proselytize the Orthodox, among others, and was anxious to have the works of Petros Arcudius published and circulated among the "heretics." Arcudius died in 1634, when Paisius was still a student. The young scholar helped to edit one of the works entitled *On the Purgatorial Fire* which appeared in 1637; in this publication the remarkable talents of the new devotee of the Roman faith are obvious in the elegant preface in which the budding author displays his learning and at the same time pays slavish homage to his benefactor Pope Urban. He describes the Pope as the "Divinity on Earth" in the dedication. He composed also an elegy to the "wise and learned Arcudius" in which he laments the death of one of the pillars of the Church of Saint Peter. The elegy is composed in the classical manner replete with ancient meter, simile, Homeric vocabulary, alliteration, and play on words. And in it he denigrates his countrymen whom he describes as "sinning and knavish schismatics." Paisius added a further short epigram again dedicated to the pontiff. What emerges from these adulatory dedications to the pope is the abject servility of one who though a Greek by birth was prepared to serve his masters blindly against what in his mind were the "heretical beliefs" of his own people.

Paisius presented his thesis on philosophy and theology on September 27, 1636, before a magnificently attired assembly of cardinals in the Church of Saint Athanasius and defended it in both Greek and Latin with an extraordinary facility of retort which did not fail to impress the stately gathering. One of those present proposed questions in Greek to which the candidate responded offhandedly with a rapidity and fullness that excited the admiration of all those present.[10] The Romans indeed had found a brilliant agent for the propagation of their faith. They had every reason to be proud of the new disciple of Saint Peter, and their investment in the young Chiote had not, at least for the moment, gone to waste.

Paisius received all his orders in the same church at the hands of Raphael Korsak, the Ruthenian metropolitan of Russia in December, 1639, and on December 31 was finally ordained a priest.

The sixteen years of schooling in Italy had produced one of the outstanding Greek theologians of the century. The young Catholic missionary, armed with the intimate knowledge of the theology of both churches, fortified by his masters in Rome both with their blessings and a generous yearly allowance, set out for the East from which he was never to return.

CHAPTER 2

The Middle Period

PAISIUS had taught in Rome for a few years before leaving for the East, and it is quite possible that he had spent some time at the famous university of Padua, which so many of his fellow islanders had attended, for further studies. He makes mention of Padua in his *Book of Prophecies,* but most scholars doubt whether he had actually studied there.

The new Catholic missionary broke his long journey to Chios by stopping at Venice where there existed the largest thriving Greek community in western Europe. It is most likely, being such a bibliophile, that he took advantage of his brief stay here to pore over the precious manuscript collection of Saint Mark, the library which had been started by the great Byzantine theologian and scholar Bessarion in the fifteenth century, soon after the fall of Constantinople. From Venice Paisius sailed to Zante, the tranquil and prosperous island affectionately known to the Venetians as "the flower of the Levant." On July 14, 1642, he wrote his first letter from abroad to his friend and mentor Leo Allatius from that island. Written in the awkward demotic Greek of the time, Paisius took the occasion to express his deep affection for Allatius and to ask for a favor:

I did not want to omit greeting your excellency, but not being able to perform my duty while in Venice, I write you now from Zante where I had the occasion to meet with his excellency the noble gentleman George Serras, our fellow-countryman. He has shown me such affection and kindness that I have become forever obligated to him. At the dinner which he gave in my honor, I brought up your excellency's name and the fine book which was written concerning the birthplace of Homer. He became so roused and anxious to read it that he begged me to write to you for a copy as a token of affection for and a reminder of our native land. I am confident that you will not fail to honor that noble personage with such a book, and it would also please me to have acted as the mediator for such a gift.

Just as in the past I have been throughout your obedient and faithful servant, so shall I continue being so in the future and for as long as I am alive, proclaiming your name wherever I may go. For indeed I am very fortunate in having such a dear and most learned friend as Leo Allatius for whom to work, and I shall preach the word throughout the whole of Greece, as is befitting.[1]

I *Return of the Native*

From Zante Paisius sailed to Chios. After an absence of nearly twenty years he had returned, but as a Catholic missionary in the pay of Rome to work for the union of the churches. The situation, however, had changed in Chios and in the East, for the Orthodox were beginning to emerge from their lethargic and passive attitude to the Catholics and to take countermeasures against the subtle and insipid penetration of the island in particular and in the Greek-speaking world in general. Indeed, the counterattack against the Jesuits and other Catholic agencies had reached its climax a few years earlier with the tragic death of Cyril Lukaris, patriarch of Constantinople, undoubtedly the greatest Greek cleric since Photius.

Paisius arrived in the agitated island at a time when the polemics between Latin and Greek clergymen had reached a feverish pitch. The Papacy had contributed much to the education of Greek youth in Chios by establishing schools for the purpose of attracting the "schismatics," but it failed to realize that this policy would inevitably lead to a reaction on the part of the Orthodox. The relationships between the two churches had been intimate and friendly in the sixteenth century, but these relationships turned sour and became more and more malicious and caustic in the course of the seventeenth century: The Turks, whose custom it was to take advantage of any disputes among the Christians, welcomed yet another opportunity to weaken the power of both churches and at the same time to fill their coffers further through the well-tried and common practice of bribery. Latin power and influence on the island decreased rapidly and eventually the Catholics became entirely dependent upon the whims of the Greeks. What little Latin influence remained at the end of the century was effaced as a result of these quarrels. Indeed, the ambitious plan of Ignatius Neochoris, Orthodox bishop of Chios, either to force the Westerners to submit to the Orthodox church or to cause the confiscation of their property, was finally realized.[2] The efforts of the Latin prelate Andrea Soffiano, appointed Catholic bishop of the island in the year before Paisius arrived to stem the onslaught of the Greek clergy, succeeded in staying the rapid decline of Latin power only temporarily.

How unreasonable and senseless can be the fanaticism of religious bigotry, and how readily are forgotten the intrinsic virtues of Christianity when the outward forms of religion determine the social behavior of a society. Such was the pattern in Chios at the time. Yet, though the Chiotes may have had a monopoly of certain commercial transactions in that region, certainly they did not have a monopoly of the malpractices and vices of the time. They cannot have been expected to be entirely free from the social errors in the age in which they lived. Toleration is a Christian virtue, but there was little religious toleration in the world of the seventeenth century, either in the East or in the more enlightened West. Moreover, religious bigotry was further aggravated by foreign interference. The Greek prelates were rightly alarmed by the inroads made by the ambassadors and agents of the Catholic powers in Constantinople who had used their political and commercial posts to spread the Roman dogma throughout both the Ottoman Empire and eastern Europe.

II *Orthodoxy vs. Catholicism*

The most tireless and aggressive zealot of Greek Orthodoxy in Chios was the learned physician and theologian George Koressios. Educated in Italy and residing in Chios, he composed many polemical tracts against both Catholics and Calvinists. These numerous works of which few have ever been published were circulated for the most part in manuscript form. Among other works by this energetic Chiote was a study of Aristotle. His attacks against the great Galileo indicate, if nothing else, the pugnacity of the man who was disliked by Cyril Lukaris, hated but respected by Leo Allatius who condemned him for his detestation of Catholicism, yet admitted his sagacity and learning, and admired by Paisius Ligarides who went so far as to compose an epigram to the "most-wise and learned Koressios" which still survives in a manuscript on Mount Athos.[3]

Paisius found himself in an awkward and unhappy situation,

torn between loyalty and duty to his benefactors in Rome and a deep-rooted affection for his compatriots and friends on the island who were in the opposite religious camp. He had received detailed instructions from Allatius while in Rome for his missionary work in Chios, and had received also a generous yearly stipend which would enable him to carry out his duties comfortably. But as a graduate of the Greek College, suspicion fell heavily upon him. The Greek Orthodox clergy and the patriarch of Constantinople himself had attacked the college in no uncertain terms as the "ruin of Greece," [4] and the latter actually issued a decree that those who had been educated there should not be received or welcomed, for they were disturbers of the peace and were open and sworn enemies of the Greek people. His situation being so uncomfortable on the island, Paisius took the coward's way out by abandoning Chios for a better and safer hunting ground.

III *Constantinople, the Second Rome*

In Constantinople the atmosphere was, if anything, more chaotic and unsettled. Paisius found himself in a boiling cauldron of intrigue involving the embassies of the foreign powers, the Greek Patriarchate, and the ever-present Turkish authorities. Nor were his relationships with the Catholics in Galata, the Christian suburb of Constantinople, very cordial.

The Patriarchate had become the arena in the long and bitter struggle in which the Catholic powers—France, Spain, Poland, Austria, and Venice—were arrayed against the Protestant powers —England, Sweden, and Holland.[5] The ecclesiastical confrontation between the Roman and Orthodox Churches, in which the pope and the patriarch were the protagonists, was but a screen behind which the political ambitions of these powers in the Levant clashed. The only real victors in the long run were the Ottoman authorities themselves.

The order of Jesuits had established a theological seminary in the old European quarter of Galata. In their struggle for the conversion of the Orthodox Greek population, the Jesuits were not overscrupulous in their methods and by the use of the potent means of bribery at the Ottoman court, they were able to win a number of concessions from the authorities. Having succeeded in eliminating their most formidable adversary, Cyril Lukaris, who was supported by the Protestant faction, the Jesuits backed the candidacy of Cyril Contaris as the new patriarch. Contaris was a Romanizer who had been educated at the Jesuit seminary of Galata, and he assumed the patriarchal throne for the third time as Cyril II, but was able to retain his position for only a year. Such was the intrigue and bribery flourishing at Constantinople that in the period from the time Paisius entered the college in Rome and the time he had arrived in Constantinople twenty years later, seven patriarchs had sat on the ecumenical throne at twelve different times.

It appears that Leo Allatius had built his hopes on the favor of Cyril II, but these hopes were soon dashed to the ground, for when Paisius arrived in the metropolis the "Latin disciple" was forced to make way for Parthenius the First. In a letter to a friend, Allatius writes, "Pantaleon Ligarides three years ago left Rome for Constantinople to visit his native isle of Scio and to diffuse in those parts the Roman faith." He adds further, "But from trustworthy information it seems that Pantaleon's affairs are not in a good way with the new patriarch, who has been raised to the chair by the heretics. O that this journey had fallen to my own lot." [6] Allatius assured his correspondent that Paisius Ligarides was even prepared to sacrifice his life for the sake of the Latin church. Such was the faith and the confidence in which he held his protégé and countryman.

Although a Greek Orthodox and uncontaminated by Jesuit teaching, the new patriarch was a rather timid cleric and much frightened by the growing power and influence of the Catholics. He was all too familiar with the fate that had awaited the great Lukaris who dared to challenge and fight the invidious and formidable enemy. And so he took no steps that would aggravate the Catholics. Paisius was thus unhindered in his efforts to secretly proselytize the Greeks of the metropolis. The report that he had defended the Latin faith openly in the city appears to be unfounded.

Ecumenical Patriarch Parthenius I gave him permission to preach, to celebrate mass, and to hear confessions. It would appear that Paisius worked as a Catholic the first year of his stay in Constantinople, but the following year when Parthenius II assumed the throne, he worked as an Orthodox. And so it is not surprising that he was considered an Orthodox by the successors of Parthenius, who in 1647 gave him patriarchal letters of recommendation as a bona fide Greek Christian for his trip to the Danubian provinces. He would not have received such letters if he had indicated his Latin beliefs in public. In any event, in his letters to Allatius from Constantinople, he presents himself still working secretly for the Papacy and at the same time asks for an increase in his yearly stipend from Rome. Paisius had developed a craving for wealth, and he never shed this unsavory aspect of his character.

Ligarides corresponded frequently with Allatius during his four-year visitation of Constantinople. In a letter dated June 6, 1643, he writes on behalf of a mutual acquaintance interested in filling the vacant Catholic bishopric of the Aegean island of Siphnos. He asks Allatius to bring the matter to the attention of the Congregation in Rome. In yet another letter of the same year he complains of the actions of a certain Dominican vicar who has misappropriated church monies and maintains a hostile attitude toward the Chiotes. Paisius begs Allatius to intercede on behalf of their fellow countrymen.

Armed with letters of recommendation from Patriarch Joannicus and fortified by an increase in his yearly allowance from Rome, the ambitious adventurer was pleased to abandon the insecure and highly competitive atmosphere of intrigue that permeated the teeming metropolis for the potentially more profitable and less cultivated regions in the Danubian basin where clerics and teachers were not as numerous and opportunities for gain were much broader for a man of his capabilities. Paisius departed hence for the North in 1647.

IV *Greener Pastures*

Wallachia and Moldavia were two principalities owing fealty to the sultan. Situated on the outer fringes of the empire, subject therefore to greater influences from the nations bordering them to the North and West, their history took a course somewhat different from that of the other Balkan nations. Yet their fate was determined by the political ambitions of those who conducted affairs in Constantinople, especially the Greeks of that city who had somehow succeeded in infiltrating every branch of the imperial administration. Indeed, it is remarkable how, though subjects and abject slaves of an odious Moslem master, they were able to move up the slippery ladder of power and influence and eventually become the diplomats, administrators, and businessmen of the Turks. This was no less true in the case of the Romanian provinces where they succeeded in ousting the native ruling families and occupied the most exalted positions in the hierarchy throughout the long period of Ottoman occupation. The fact that the Wallachian and Moldavian inhabitants of that region had a common form of religion with the Greeks contributed much to the easy infiltration and domination of the Danubian principalities by the Greek administrators, merchants, and clergymen.

The Ottomans appointed and dismissed princes of these border regions with such frequency, as in the case of the ecumenical patriarchs, that there were six reigns in Wallachia and ten in Moldavia in less than twenty years. And these appointments and dismissals were made by the Greeks of the capital who became very adept at the sale of such moneymaking positions as the crowns of Moldavia and Wallachia. They had learned their lesson well in the Ottoman school of bribery. To retain these crowns, the various *voivodes* (princes) were compelled to pay homage first to the Greek and second to the Turkish men of influence in Constantinople.[7]

When Paisius entered the region which was to preoccupy him for fifteen years—except for a brief interval of two years spent in the Holy Land—the Romanian provinces had been enjoying a short but vigorous administration of two remarkable princes who in many ways were responsible for the revival of learning in the area.[8] The colorful Basil Lupu, or Basil "the Wolf" (1634–53), ruled in Moldavia and the equally interesting Matthew Bassarab held the crown of Wallachia. To remain in the good graces of the Sultan, they had to satisfy their Greek advisers; to pacify the latter, it was essential that they be generous and cooperative with Greeks residing in Romania.

Bassarab of Wallachia and Basil of Moldavia inaugurated an era of general culture in Romania. The former established the first printing press in Bucharest, and the first publication in the Romanian language on Romanian soil appeared in 1640. The latter founded a printing press in a monastery of Jassy from which emerged a volume of sermons in 1643.[9] Dominantly theological and legal, these books appeared in Greek, Latin, Slavonic, and Romanian. Besides the printing presses the vying princes founded schools in Bucharest, Targovişte, and Jassy, in which were taught

Greek, Latin, Slavonic and native tongues. A large number of the teachers and editors were of necessity Greek.

It is a pity indeed that Bassarab and Basil were deadly enemies. They rivaled one another not only in the arts of peace but in the techniques of political intrigue and war, and each sought outside intervention to promote his own ambitions. Their subjects paid a heavy price for these ambitions, for when Basil and Bassarab passed from the scene in 1654, the principalities with their unfortunate inhabitants relapsed into their former unhappy state of servitude and passivity. Yet the harm that the two rulers brought to the country was counterbalanced by the great advance in learning, and Romania's beginnings in cultural development date from this era. In this renaissance of learning the Greeks played not a small part. Chios again supplied a large number of intellectuals both within the empire and without.[10]

The first visit to the Danubian provinces which lasted four years was in many ways an exploratory one. We find Paisius initially at the ancient capital town of Targovişte situated in the foothills of the Transylvanian Alps some forty-five miles northwest of Bucharest. Here existed a school and a printing press that had been newly founded by Bassarab. Appointed court chaplain and confessor to that prince, Paisius lost no time in enriching himself as priest, theologian, and teacher. He composed various sermons including attacks against the Lutherans and Calvinists who had succeeded in making threatening inroads into Transylvania and Wallachia. By concentrating his polemics against the western "Reformers," he was able to lay a smoke screen to divert any suspicions that may have arisen concerning his Catholicism. During this very active period in Romania the adroit cleric continued to receive his allowance from Rome.

With his compatriot Ignatius Petritzes, he helped to edit the first book of canonical law to be published in Wallachia. There had been an urgent need for such a publication and the project was undertaken by a certain monk Daniel under the auspices of Bassarab. Encountering difficulties with the Greek text and sources, Daniel had recourse to the Chiote luminaries Paisius and Petritzes. The book finally came off the press at Targovişte on March 22, 1652, after Paisius had departed for other climes, but his contribution was acknowledged. In the introduction to the edition containing 795 pages of text and 25 prefatory pages, Daniel remarks that he was assisted by "Ignatius Petritzes and Panteleimon Ligarides, excellent masters, both of Chios, renowned and versed in all the sacred writings." [11]

Petritzes, who also taught at Tergoviste with Paisius, was the learned monk who was to put into rhyme a version of the great medieval epic *Digenes Akrites,* the manuscript of which now survives at Oxford.[12] This manuscript had been purchased by the English traveler Wheler, of Spon and Wheler fame. Petritzes humanizes the story, which is well proportioned and not savage, and is set in a more refined world. Priests and bishops, for example, are introduced to celebrate funerals and weddings while the Arabs become Turks. The lengthy masterpiece of popular epic set in the "political" or fifteen-syllable rhyming verse of medieval Greek, was completed by the Chiote monk on November 25, 1670, just before his death.[13]

It was probably during this first visit to Tergoviste that Paisius, the insatiable connoisseur of rare books, saw in manuscript the *History of Wallachia* by the metropolitan, Matthew of Myra, composed in beautifully flowing fifteen-syllable demotic Greek verse and dated 1615. The history was not published until long after Matthew's death.[14] From this manuscript Paisius cites a passage which he incorporates in the *Book of Prophecies.* Matthew decries the faith which the Greeks put in oracular utterances and in eventual help from other nations for liberation from the Turks:

> We place our hopes in the actions of Spain
> And on the heavy ships of the Venetian main,
> Who will come with the sword to slay the Turk
> And recover our kingdom and give it to us.
> We also hope in the race of the North
> To come down from Moscow to liberate us.
> We believe in oracles and vain predictions,
> We waste our time with prognostications.
> We look to the North, in the winds for hope
> To release the bonds of the Turkish yoke.[15]

The last four verses are quoted by Paisius in his prologue to the *Book of Prophecies* in which he protests against the pessimistic views of Metropolitan Matthew and his disbelief in prognostication.

From Wallachia Paisius moved on to Moldavia where he taught

theology and philosophy at the Jassy Academy established by Basil Lupu. We find the adventurer and opportunist shifting from one principality to the next, getting involved no doubt in the political machinations of the rival rulers, playing one against the other, settling for the more lucrative, and exploiting their mutual animosity to obtain the greatest possible personal gain. The hostility between Wallachian and Moldavian princes reached its climax at this time and a large sector of the native population began to turn against the Greeks, whom they viewed as intruders and plotters undermining their national aspirations. Experienced in such intrigues, foreseeing the impasse to which developments were leading, Paisius found the opportunity to slip out of the explosive situation. This opportunity came in the form of a timely meeting with two visiting dignitaries, the famous Russian monk and traveller Arsenij Souchanov and Patriarch Paisius of Jerusalem. These two personages were destined to play a decisive role in the chain of events that marked the subsequent career of Paisius Ligarides.

The Russian theologian Souchanov had been dispatched from Moscow on a mission to collect liturgical books from the various Greek monasteries, the purpose being to obtain reliable texts for the correction of Russian liturgical practices which had deviated considerably from those of the original faith. From Mount Athos he was to bring back to Moscow 500 ecclesiastical manuscripts and books on the basis of which the Russian texts were eventually corrected. Of these, 156 codices were from the monastery of Iveron alone. In 1660, sixteen years later, the same monastery sent an additional 14 codices to Moscow. Souchanov became intimate with Ligarides whom he accompanied on his trip to Palestine, while the Patriarch of Jerusalem was so impressed with the learning of Paisius that he was happy to take him to Jerusalem when the wily Chiote so proposed. The time for departure from the troubled principalities of Romania was at hand, and so the three odd traveling companions, one a secret agent of the papacy, another a Russian monk in quest of manuscripts and liturgical books, and the third, the "most divine and holy lord, the Lord Patriarch of the Holy City Jerusalem and of the whole Land of Promise," set off for the see of Saint James.

CHAPTER 3

The Final Phase

THE see of Saint James, the "brother of God," always has been the poorest of the four ancient patriarchates of the eastern church.[1] Within its jurisdiction fall thirteen dioceses extending across Palestine and the Sinai Peninsula, the only exception being the isolated monastic community of Saint Catherine in the Sinai Desert, which enjoys a unique autonomy. Today there are an estimated sixty thousand people who obey the Orthodox patriarch.[2] Since the fifteenth century all the patriarchs have been Greeks, although the Orthodox flock is for the most part composed of Syrian Arabs. In the brief period that Paisius spent in Jerusalem, enormous sums of money were beginning to flow into the holy site, particularly from Russia and the Danubian provinces. Indeed, the czars of Russia continued as generous benefactors of the see until as late as the Bolshevik Revolution in 1917. The patriarch had been visiting the Romanian principalities for donations and gifts when he met with Paisius, and it is very likely that the latter was attracted to the Holy Land by the possibilities for further personal enrichment.

The patriarch, in any event, was much impressed by the Chiote. Moreover, the Orthodox church was desperately in need of learned theologians, and the patriarch no doubt believed that Paisius would be a useful addition to a church in dire need of intellectuals of his caliber. Furthermore, Paisius had expressed the desire to work for the cause of orthodoxy and for the church of Jerusalem in particular. Soon after his arrival in Palestine, on Sunday, November 16, the patriarch tonsured Ligarides as an Orthodox monk in the Church of the Resurrection. At that time, his worldly name was changed from Panteleimon to Paisius in honor of his patron, who obviously did not suspect that he was tonsuring a Catholic priest. Their Russian friend, Arsenij Souchanov, acted as the novice monk's spiritual sponsor and novice master.[3] Disguised in Orthodox garb, the papal agent could henceforth work for the Roman church with greater freedom.

I *The First Manuscript*

It is not surprising that, with the numerous manuscripts available in the patriarchal library, Paisius should become preoccupied with writing a *History of the Patriarchs of Jerusalem.* So potent still was his Catholic discipline that it was written from the Latin point of view. Years later, when the new patriarch assumed the throne of Saint James, the contents became known, and both the work and the author were condemned. Dositheus, the brilliant theologian and pillar of the eastern church, who subsequently became a patriarch, made great use of this manuscript and acknowledged his debt to Paisius when he wrote his own history of the patriarchs of Jerusalem. According to Dositheus,

> Paisius Ligarides of Chios, a Latinizer, who wrote an interpretation of the divine liturgy with Roman innovations, also wrote a *History of the Patriarchs of Jerusalem* in 83 folios by which my present work was much benefited. In the history he wrote of the patriarchs up to Heraclius; and after the reign of Heraclius he wrote nothing favorably about them. A third part of the history concerns the ascetics and the patriarchs. The two sections were against the Eastern Church, in particular against the divine Photius, and on behalf of the primacy of the Pope. When his history was read by Patriarch Methodius of Constantinople and Nectarius of Jerusalem and they detected the extreme blasphemy of the contents, they anathematized the book and excommunicated Ligarides as a heretic.[4]

It is indeed regrettable that the eighty three folio pages have not survived, although some of the contents may have been incorporated in Paisius's *Book of Prophecies.*

II *Higher Ambitions*

It was probably while writing the history that the ambitions of the novitiate monk soared high and he fancied himself as patriarch of the ancient see itself. He persuaded the unsuspecting patriarch to ordain him deacon, then priest, and finally archbishop of Gaza. To dispel any suspicions regarding his orthodoxy, and to forestall any accusations of "Romanizing" that may have arisen, Paisius composed a confession of faith before the actual ceremony of ordination: "Since certain informants do not cease to accuse me of Latinizing and believing in the Pope and papal dogmas and teachings, I hereby make the following confession of faith."

In the statement he swears adherence to the five patriarchs of the eastern church and to Moscow.[5] The ceremony of ordination took place on September 14, 1652, in the Church of the Holy Sepulcher. Henceforth, Paisius would sign his sermons, letters, and works, as "The most holy and wise Archbishop of Gaza, Lord Paisius." In an extant letter to the Protosyncellus and subsequent Metropolitan Cosmas, Paisius describes the great event which was in many ways the turning point of his entire career.[6] In the impressive Byzantine ceremony, he recited the Nicene Creed or confession of faith and swore adhesion to the four Patriarchs of the eastern Orthodox church.[7] An Englishman by name of Basire was present at the ceremony and he reported that Ligarides solemnly recited the credo, denounced Roman Catholicism, and stamped his feet thrice on an icon depicting the seven hills of Rome and the double-headed eagle. Franciscan monks who were also present were shocked by the scandalous behavior of the papal agent, but, unperturbed, the new archbishop immediately after the ceremony hastened to the Latin hostelry and asserted, again in the presence of the Englishman Basire, that despite the ceremony of ordination and the recitation of the creed in the Church of the Holy Sepulcher, he remained and would always remain firm and loyal to the Church of Rome. But the Latin monks would not hear of this, and after his departure from the hostelry, they described the Chiote to Basire as a "notorious hypocrite." [8]

Word of the actions of the new archbishop soon reached Rome and understandably papal circles were shocked by these reports. Rome summoned Paisius to report, but the clever clergyman protested his innocence loudly and insisted that he continued to work for the interests of the papacy. Indeed, he expressed his astonishment that those in Rome could possibly believe that he was Orthodox. In Constantinople, meanwhile, Ecumenical Patriarch Joannicus had received from Ligarides an autograph copy of his Orthodox confession of faith. The Capuchin monk Thomas, vicar in Constantinople, was much distressed by this document, a copy of which he managed to obtain after Joannicus had vacated the throne with the promise that it would be returned. The signature of Ligarides on the original was identified beyond a doubt as authentic by two Capuchin acquaintances, John Franciscus and Jacob of Paris, by the Catholic missionary and former fellow student Andreas Stavrinos, and by Antonius Timonis, a former pupil of Ligarides at the Greek College in Rome.[9] Despite the overwhelming evidence of proselytization, Paisius appears to have convinced those in Rome that he was still working in the interests of the papacy. Indeed, he went so far as to use his Orthodox title when writing to the propaganda and demanding payment of arrears. The yearly stipend continued to arrive, and it is highly probable that Ligarides now played the role of the Catholic agent solely for the annual allowance, which he used to support his family and relatives in Chios.

III *Early Sermons*

While in Jerusalem, the newly ordained archbishop delivered twelve significant sermons before the patriarch, of which eleven survive in a manuscript to be found in Athens.[10] His florid panegyric style and language had improved considerably since he left Rome. In these sermons, more like orations, the master of rhetoric uses a simple language to interpret the twelve feast days of the Orthodox calendar. The eleven surviving pieces are very representative of his exquisite Greek, wide learning, and Orthodox beliefs, which now begin to sound more convincing and sincere.[11] We also detect in these sermons an almost overbearing conceit and elation indicative of a gloating self-satisfaction. The cycle of "Paisian" sermons, as the author designates them, is prefaced by an imaginative and original comparison between the twelve zodiacal signs and the twelve feast days. In this preface the prelate displays a considerable knowledge of and a fondness for astrological phenomena :"The sign of Virgo arose when the angel Gabriel came to the city of Nazareth announcing the arrival of the Messiah." Then, in his customary immodest manner and with the usual fawning flattery in addressing the patriarch, the author adds: "And behold, I too now flash and thunder for the lightning word of the Spirit, like a new Pericles."

There exist several curious scholia or comments by later readers of the sermons written in the margins of the manuscript. One particular comment is a criticism of an interpretation made by Paisius and reads: "Well, your Dionysian enumeration is erroneous, and your Paisian continuity false when you maintain that on the fifteenth day of the moon the Last Supper took place, and the crucifixion of Christ on the sixteenth."

It is significant that these orations contain on the whole no Romanizing tendencies. On the contrary, they are very Orthodox in conception and content and are critical of Roman teaching. Nevertheless, it is difficult to dismiss or obliterate one's early formative schooling, and the Archbishop makes every conscious effort to avoid the pernicious influence which here and there emerges in his sermons. We find, for example, an over-adulation of the Virgin Mary, or *Mariolatry,* to the point of deification, which was a common Roman practice. Moreover, the author cites many western theologians who were for the most part unknown to the Greeks of the eastern church. As we shall see, his western background emerges very strongly in the *Book of Prophecies* wherein quotations from Catholic authorities and theologians abound.

Another curious sermon in this cycle contains a fairly detailed description of the Church of the Resurrection in the Holy Sepulcher which is of some historical and literary merit since the church was completely destroyed by fire on September 30, 1808, reputedly by an Armenian monk, and rebuilt two years later. It brings to mind the Byzantine ecphrasis or description, a form used by Procopius in prose and Paul the Silentiary in verse to describe the Church of the Holy Wisdom in sixth-century Constantinople.

The Russian Souchanov left Jerusalem on April 27, 1652, a few months before Paisius was ordained metropolitan.[12] He had visited Chios briefly on his journey to Palestine earlier, and we hear of him again on the Holy Mountain, from which he carried Greek manuscripts and liturgical books to Moscow in 1654. Souchanov was to be instrumental in having Paisius invited officially to Moscow by Nicon, the great Russian patriarch, three years later when the Chiote had deserted Jerusalem for the Danubian provinces.

The economically poor see of Saint James offered limited opportunities for personal enrichment, even for an archbishop, and Paisius became restless and began to feel the need for greener pastures. It would appear also that his hopes for eventually succeeding the patriarch of Jerusalem quickly evaporated. Perhaps the patriarch had begun to suspect the integrity and character of the ambitious and newly ordained prelate, and in any case the wealth of the Danubian principalities was too tempting and beckoning for a cleric of such lofty ecclesiastical rank to tarry any longer in the needy Palestinian see. Moreover, he could use his exalted title to seek alms for the Holy Land and appropriate these donations for personal use. Paisius therefore gathered his books, manuscripts, and priestly accouterments, and set off for the North never to return to his metropolitan see. His chance meeting with the patriarch on his first visit to the Romanian provinces and his brief interlude in Jerusalem had provided him with a formidable title that would be put to maximum use.

CHAPTER 4

Retracing of Steps

THE forty-four-year-old prelate took the overland route through Aleppo where he halted briefly to deliver a sermon in the Orthodox cathedral.[1] Always nostalgic for his beloved birthplace, Paisius interrupted the journey northward to spend a few months in Chios before embarking for the Ottoman metropolis and hastening to the Romanian provinces. From Chios he wrote several letters, which are still extant, to his loyal friend and compatriot Leo Allatius in Rome. The earliest is a panegyric to that remarkable man of letters with the opening, "O most wise and dearly beloved Leo Allatius, thou sweet salt of wisdom and divine," wherein he indulges in his favorite practice of word play, likening Allatius to the salt of the earth, and using the occasion to remind him of his patriotic obligation and promise to donate his rich private library to Chios.[2] It is possible that the Catholics of the island objected to this plan, although the letter does not identify the parties that were hostile to the idea. This letter, written in Greek, was sent in the early part of the year soon after his arrival in Chios.[3]

A second letter, written in Italian, and dated April 13, 1654, again reminds Allatius of his promise:

I could not write nor would I have written to your excellency, but I was asked to do so by the Society of Saints Cosmas and Damian concerning your inspired idea about the library, and because you have always shown your kindness to me. As for your library, I am convinced that you will be performing an act which is in keeping with your reputation, since to leave this library in Rome is so much like carrying coals to Newcastle.[4] And I assure you that I was overwhelmed, believe me, by the piety, the magnificence and philanthropy that I saw in Chios this Lent. There are three Greek societies, so numerous, so wealthy, that each has more than a thousand members (not including women), and all these take Holy Communion on every feast day of the Virgin.

Moreover, they do so much Christian teaching, perform so many pious acts and have so many schools that it would be difficult to believe if you did not see it. I do not speak of the Latins, since you know all about them. Suffice it to say that there is a Christian emulation, not in words, but very visible, a harmony not the slightest removed from the original faith of the church. And the person who said that "the Chiote is an evil man" has been proven false.[5]

While enjoying the congenial climate of Chios with his family and friends (he was never to set foot on the island again), the restless Ligarides lost no time in slandering the very patriarch who had shortly before entrusted him with the see of Gaza. It was probably during this visit that he composed several epigrams to the "most learned George Koressios," the doctor, theologian, and militant foe of the Catholics, who was doing so much to check the inroads made in the island by papist missionaries. The epigrams survive in manuscript form on Mount Athos.[6]

I *Back to Constantinople*

The nomadic prelate next disembarked at Constantinople where the chronically chaotic condition of the church had gone from bad to worse. The forty-year reign of Sultan Mohammed IV (1648–87) had already begun. In the meantime, the rapid pace of changes in the Patriarchate had gathered momentum. Joannicus II occupied the ecumenical throne for the third time and retained it for eight months, only to be replaced by Cyril III who sat on the throne for the second time, but for a brief two weeks. Paisius I succeeded him for a period of one year and was followed by Joannicus II, who again assumed his see for the fourth time and was not to retire for the relatively long period of sixteen months (March, 1655, until the middle of July, 1656). In the preface to his *Book of Prophecies,* Ligarides relates that "Cyril, the Patriarch of Constantinople, informed me that he had read that the Agar [that is to say, the Turk] whose name began with an 'M' would lose Constantinople which was conquered by Mohammed whose name also begins with 'M,' just as a Constantine founded Constantinople and Constantine Paleologue lost it." [7] In the mind of Paisius, as in the thoughts of many Greeks, the time for the liberation of the race appeared very propitious because a Mohammed had become the reigning sultan. This passage, however, raises the question of the date of his arrival in the Ottoman capital, for Cyril was Patriarch for only fourteen days (in March), and Ligarides could not possibly have arrived in Constantinople until some months later, since his letter to Allatius from Chios bears the date April 13, 1654. If, in fact, the author did hear the remark from Cyril, it would indicate that he met the ecumenical patriarch after he had vacated the throne. In any event, Paisius found the atmosphere of the capital uncongenial and hastened his departure for the "happier hunting grounds" beyond the Danube.

II *The Danubian Principalities*

We next encounter the vagabond metropolitan in the Romanian principalities. The situation in these areas was but a reflection of the unsettled conditions reigning throughout the continent. With the possible exception of England under the Protectorate of Oliver Cromwell, all Europe was suffering under the scourge of universal war. Germany lay prostrate as a result of the ravages of the Thirty Years' War. France, where Louis XIV had started his long reign, was locked in deadly conflict with the Spain of Philip IV, while the Ottoman Empire and Venice wrestled for the strategic island of Crete. Poles, Mongols, Cossacks, Danes, Swedes, and Russians were all interlocked in common conflict, while insurrections in the subject provinces of Turkey were undermining that country. The Ottoman Empire, however, was fortunate in having at its helm the able grand vizier and devoted leader Mehmet Kiuprulu, who succeeded in reviving temporarily the prestige of the sublime porte by restoring discipline in the army and strengthening the administration, which had reverted to a large degree into the hands of Greeks and other subject races. Thanks to his dynamic leadership, the Empire recovered some of its former strength and was able to go over to the offensive. The Turk was strong only when on the march: in times of peace and military inactivity he had a tendency to become inefficient, slothful, and corrupt. And so the second half of the seventeenth century was marked by a partial revival of Ottoman power.

When Paisius Ligarides arrived on his second and last visit to the principalities, Matthew Bassarab and Basil Lupu had passed from the scene. Constantine Bassarab, or the "Camus," now held the Wallachian crown, whereas George Stephen governed Moldavia. The neighboring province of Transylvania, which had become the battleground for Hungarian and German ambitions, was at the same time a springboard for Lutheran teaching and infiltration of the Romanian provinces. Indeed, the Lutherans had established a strong foothold in that mountainous region. It was at this time that Paisius composed many polemical tracts against the Protestant dogma for the benefit of those numerous Romanians of Transylvania who had proselytized. These surviving exhortations or sermons to return to the true Orthodox faith still remain unpublished.

The position of the Greeks in the area had been further strengthened. Turkish sovereignty and Greek culture were the two dominant elements that determined the course of its history. Greek culture in fact had all but ousted what little Slavic influence had managed to survive. The Ottoman administration, strongly permeated by the energetic Greek element in the capital, continued to act as mediator, prince-maker, and bribe receiver. The Greeks directed their energies into two basic channels: the church, which had become the strongest bulwark of racial identity, and commerce, which provided the economic weapons for political dominance. The Sultan's merchants, bankers, interpreters, and political advisers were Greek for the most part. This race thus acquired the means by which it could fill the vacancies in both church and civil administration with its coreligionists. By the middle of the seventeenth century, with their natural aptitude for commerce, fondness for travel, adventurous spirit, and exceptional linguistic abilities, the Greeks dominated the wealthy and profitable principalities both economically and politically.

A certain Panayotakis Nicoussis, also of Chios, who was so representative of this circle of Greeks in Constantinople, had become indispensable to the sublime porte. He first proposed the establishment of the office of the grand dragoman (interpreter). Through his hands would pass all official documents from foreign powers, and in this manner the holder of the office became the focal point of diplomatic negotiations between the Ottoman Empire and the European powers. A Greek proverb was circulating in the latter half of the seventeenth century which said that it was as hard to come across a green horse as a wise man in the island of Chios, and so Panayotakis was known ironically as the "Green Horse." [8] This ambitious and competent Chiote often accompanied Grand Vizier Mehmet Kiuprulu on his campaigns against the Venetians, Austrians, or Russians. He was instrumental in bringing the negotiations for the surrender of Candia (Crete) by Venice to a happy conclusion.[9] The same Panayotakis, a few years later, was to forbid the re-entry of Paisius into the Ottoman Empire from Russia as an undesirable.

The custom, at this time, of dedicating new monasteries to such great centers of the Orthodox faith as Mount Sinai, Jerusalem, and Mount Athos, was firmly established. In the Jassy area alone, in Moldavia, four such monastic establishments were owned by the Holy Sepulcher of Jerusalem. Control of these monasteries and convents also fell into the hands of the Greek clergy, and their incomes were regularly sent to those centers outside Romania. Greek, too, became the language of intellectuals and of the princely houses of the Danubian provinces.

III *Political Intrigue*

Paisius had his first appointment at the Jassy Academy, but soon the intriguing archbishop became involved with the political ambitions of the ruling princes. His seven years' visitation of the Romanian principalities was a series of triumphs, in the literary and economic sense, but of disasters in the political arena. He found himself inextricably involved in the affairs of Constantine of Wallachia and his Moldavian contemporary George Stephen, men who were equally devoid of administrative ability and whose policies led to final disaster as much for themselves as for their unfortunate subjects. When an alliance was formed between Stephen and Constantine, together with the Hungarians of Transylvania against the Turk, an alliance that was to arouse the wrath of the Turk and lead to the deposition of both princes, Paisius felt sufficiently compromised not to think himself safe in Wallachia until the invasion of the Turks and Tartars was over. He fled after the dethroned princes to Hungary where he was robbed of all his possessions including the precious copy of his *Book of Prophecies*.[10] The vengeful Turks led by their grand vizier ravaged the southern part of Transylvania, and once again the unhappy Wallachians paid the price for the intrigues of an ambitious ruler. After the departure of the Ottomans, Paisius returned to Wallachia, although there exists a report that he actually moved on to Poland where he spent a long time under the Polish king, saying mass in their Catholic cathedrals; but this seems improbable.[11]

The famous Turkish traveler of the seventeenth century, Evliya

Cheleby, describes among his many journeys a raid into Transylvania at about this time (1660). Evliya enjoys the forays into Christian territory which yielded much booty in slaves and plunder.[12] It is quite possible that Paisius encountered one of these marauding bands in Transylvania that stripped him of his possessions and the original *Book of Prophecies.*

The *Book of Prophecies* is undoubtedly the most important work of Paisius Ligarides. He had gathered the contents in every country and from many authors, and finally completed the book in the Romanian provinces. The only manuscript which has come down to us in its entirety is now in Jerusalem and owes its survival to the chance meeting of Paisius and Macarius, Patriarch of Antioch, in the monastery of Kosia. There exist also a much shorter version of the work consisting of extracts, as well as a rendering in Slavic made in Moscow by a Nicolas Spatharius in 1673. Internal evidence indicates that the work had been completed by 1655 at which time Ligarides was in Moldavia. The dedication and prefatory remarks were appended by the Chiote in 1656 when he called upon Czar Alexis of Russia to liberate the enslaved Greeks.

It was after his first flight from Jassy in Moldavia to Wallachia that Paisius taught briefly in Bucharest and again visited Tergoviste and the nearby convent of Kosia. This isolated monastic retreat was the meeting place between Paisius and the peregrinating Patriarch of Antioch, who was then homeward bound from Moscow with his son, Archdeacon Paul. The latter recorded the adventures they had suffered in a curious book which has been translated from Arabic into English and French. On his encounter with Paisius, Archdeacon Paul writes:

We obtained, moreover, from the aforesaid Metropolitan of Gaza, another book in Greek, the contents of which he had gathered from every country and from many authors. He had named it the "Book of Oracles"; and it was perfectly unique, there being no other copy of it whatever in existence. Its contents were, Prophecies from the Prophets, predictions of the Wise Men, and denunciation of the Saints, in the matters foretold them concerning the events in the East brought about by the children of Hagar [that is to say, the Turks], and concerning Constantinople, and their capture of that city; things of very great curiosity, as regarding the past; and likewise their prophecies of the prepared and predestined dispositions of the future. Of this book I had two copies taken by the same writer; but it was after encountering great difficulty in persuading the proprietor to give it us to copy; for he, that is, the Metropolitan of Gaza, was altogther unwilling, until we gained his consent by several presents, and shamed him into the liberality of allowing us to do so. Every person looking into this precious book is wrapt in wonder at its prophecies, sayings and other contents. Afterwards the said prelate sent us a letter from this country, informing us, that when he was in the country of the Majars, they had plundered him, and taken everything he had; and among other things, they had robbed him of this very book. Praise be to God, who was so pleased to inspire us with His Grace, to exert our diligence in taking a copy of it; for otherwise it would have been lost to the world, and the Metropolitan's labour on it would have been uselessly expended. He sent to entreat us that we would get him a copy of it written, to supply his loss; and to God be all glory, always and for ever, in all circumstances, Amen! [13]

Paisius was persuaded to lend the travelers the book, but obviously for a price. And so Macarius found a Chiote priest, by name Baba Yani, who was a good writer, to copy out the entire manuscript. Archdeacon Paul describes how they persuaded Baba Yani to undertake the arduous task. "As the love of wine is an innate propensity of the true-born Greek," he writes, they inspirited the compatriot of Ligarides with a daily ration of wine and "his sense was sobered, and his powers of mind shone forth in all their brightness, and by the power of God he finished the book." [14] This passage refers to a rare *Book of Psalms* which the wine-addicted priest copied for the visiting prelate, but we can be sure that the *Book of Prophecies* was written in the same manner. Two okas of wine daily (about two and a half kilos) did not, to judge by the manuscript, affect the calligraphy of the cleric, although there are certain pages which indicate that his hand was not as steady in the evenings as in the mornings.

Archdeacon Paul also states that Paisius had written a brief preface to the Book of Psalms, of which no other copy existed in the world, "at the beginning and the end of which, the aforesaid Metropolitan of Gaza placed a titlepage, giving this account and explanation; viz. that, under circumstances, when this invaluable treasure was hidden, et cetera, the Creator sent the Father and Lord Patriarch, Kyr Macarius of Antioch and his son, to discover it and bring it forth, to the attainment of their premium and reward in heaven, and to the benefit of the whole Christian church, et cetera." [15]

Baba Yani had copied the *Book of Prophecies* in 1657, and this copy was taken by the Patriarch and his son Paul to Aleppo, which city they reached on April 21, 1659, after a perilous odyssey to Russia in search of alms. The brave traveling companions had traversed the Balkans and the length of Russia at a time when that part of the world was fraught with dangers from marauding bands, Tatars, Cossacks, Turks, and mercenary armies, and from the harsh winters and flooding streams so characteristic of those regions. The perilous journey had lasted seven years. But the patriarch of Antioch was not to enjoy an undisturbed peace in his see, for he was to be summoned to Moscow by Czar Alexis six years later to take part in a synod in which Paisius Ligarides and Nicon, the patriarch of Moscow, were to play the leading roles.[16]

In 1657, a year after he had written his dedication to Czar Alexis in Wallachia, and a copy had been made of his *Book of Prophecies* by the Chiote priest Baba Yani, Paisius received in December a pressing invitation from Nicon, the Russian patriarch, to come to Moscow. The Russian had learned of the scholarly reputation of the wandering prelate from Arsenij Souchanov, and having need of Greeks of intelligence, he wrote to him: "We have heard of thy learning from the monk Arsenij, and that thou wishest to see us, the great hossoudar: therefore we also wish to receive thee with affection, as our son beloved in the Holy Ghost. Only, on receiving this our letter, do thy diligence to come to the capital city of Moscow."[17]

That same month Nicon also wrote to Stephen of Moldavia, Constantine of Wallachia, and the Metropolitans of Souceava and Wallachia, asking them to facilitate his going to Moscow. But Paisius did not respond to this invitation immediately, for he was not to arrive in Moscow until five years after the urgent request had been made. It is also probable that Paisius had fled into Hungary because of his involvement in the intrigues of the Romanian voivodes or princes, and did not find the moment propitious for departure. When he finally appeared in the Russian capital, Nicon's position had changed entirely, for the dynamic and controversial patriarch had incurred the wrath of the czar.

The affairs of the itinerant archbishop were not in a very happy state. He continued to maintain his ties with Rome while composing homilies against the Lutherans and Calvinists in Wallachia and Transylvania. In the meantime, in distant Jerusalem, the new patriarch, Nectarius, defrocked and excommunicated the renegade archbishop who had absented himself from his see of Gaza since 1654. But it appears that there had been no very great publicity given to this excommunication either at Constantinople or in Moldavia. Paisius was probably summoned to Jerusalem to give an account of himself, but he allowed judgment to go by default.[18] Unable under the circumstances to obtain letters of reference from the holy see of Saint James, he somehow persuaded Ecumenical Patriarch Parthenius to give him his official blessing for the Russian trip. Nectarius in the meanwhile had reached the Danubian provinces on a quest for alms and a visit to the monastic properties of the Holy Sepulcher in Moldavia. The time of departure was obviously at hand, for Paisius was not in the least anxious to encounter the prelate who had defrocked him. Moreover, the patriarch would surely expose him to the grandees and the clergy of the principalities. The elusive Chiote therefore made haste to depart for Moscow, a full five years after receiving Nicon's pressing invitation to come.

CHAPTER 5

Moscow: The Third Rome

NICON was unquestionably the greatest character in the history of Russian church. Indeed, few could rank with him even in the long annals of the Eastern Orthodox Church. Perhaps only Chrysostom in the fourth century, Photius in the ninth, and Lukaris in the seventeenth could be ranked above him as ecclesiastical reformers and statesmen. Nicon was in many respects a Russian Chrysostom, Luther, and Wolsey all rolled into one. He was responsible for inaugurating a reform of the church, the repercussions of which were to shake the very foundations of Russia for over two centuries. It was with this ecclesiastical goliath that Paisius Ligarides was to come face to face. The wily Chiote was to be the main instrument of that faction in the Russian capital which sought to destroy the imperious reformer, much to the chagrin and discomfiture of the majority of the Greeks in the Ottoman Empire who held Nicon in the highest esteem.

I *The Russian Reformation*

Nicon's intellect and devotion to reform were matched by his commanding figure, for he stood all of seven feet in height.[1] His imposing stature crowned by an extraordinarily large head, his caustic humor and indefatigable energy tempered by a primitive obstinacy and savage spirit, terrified his enemies who were legion, and overawed his friends, who were few in number. The Russian church, which had strayed from the path of the original pristine faith of the fathers, had become perverted by strange practices introduced by a nascent clergy. The services were adulterated by unjustified alterations, and its administration undermined by insubordination to ecclesiastical authority. The corruption and decay, together with the disreputable practices of the nobility and the clergy, fired Nicon with an unquenchable zeal for reform and drove him headlong into battle against popular superstition, assertions of secular supremacy, and dissipation of the monks and clergy. This first and greatest of Russian reformers saw that the time had come for giving life to the ceremonial observances and a moral direction to the devotional aspects of Orthodox worship. With unflagging severity and indomitable courage he set out upon the difficult path to uproot the abuses of the Russian hierarchy of which the most common was drunkenness. "His janizaries are perpetually going the rounds of the city and whenever they find any priest or monk in a state of intoxication," writes the Archdeacon Paul, "he is taken to prison. We saw his prisons full of them in the most wretched condition, galled with heavy chains and logs of wood on their necks and legs." [2] Nor did the uncompromising patriarch spare the higher clergy. "When any of the higher clergy or a superior of a monastery has committed a crime, he is sentenced to irons and condemned to sift flour for the bakehouse day and night till he has completed his sentence; and in this condition we used to see them. Whereas formerly the Siberian convents were empty, this Patriarch has filled them with the heads of monasteries and higher clergy and with dissolute and wretched monks. He has been so much enraged against many of the clergy that he has had their hair shaved off and has banished them, with their wives and families, to Siberia, there to end their days in misery." [3]

The raging patriarch, on the other hand, showed unbounded munificence by founding hospitals, refuges for widows, and shelters for orphans and the aged. He visited prisons and released the inmates, if he found they had been unjustly incarcerated. Icons or sacred pictures, which in his judgment were venerated in an idolatrous manner, were removed or destroyed.[4] All icons that were painted in the Latin fashion: if the figures were correctly drawn in the western style, they were seized, their eyes poked out and then ignominiously broken on the church floor or thrown into a fire.[5] A great lover of buildings and monuments, he expended vast sums to set up new churches and monasteries. The patriarchal palace in the Kremlin is his work.

Nicon launched his ambitious program of reform by beginning with the sacred books. A number of errors, misspellings, and faulty translations had gradually crept into the Russian liturgical tomes. Teams of monks and learned scholars, foremost among these being Souchanov, the "godfather" of Paisius, were dispatched to the Greek monastic establishments and libraries in the Ottoman Empire for copies of the Greek originals from which the Russian texts were made. This entailed also the assistance of Greek scholars and theologians, and among many others, as we have seen, Paisius was asked to come to Moscow for this purpose. Greek and Latin were taught for the first time in Russian schools. Nicon, in fact, was inordinately fond of all things Greek. "I am a Russian and the son of a Russian," he was wont to say, "but my faith and my religion are Grecian." [6] For publication of the revised and corrected sacred books, he set the printing presses in motion. Some changes he introduced in the outward forms of the liturgy were that people should make fewer prostrations during service, sing "Alleluia" thrice instead of two times in the ceremony, and make the sign of the cross with three instead of with two fingers.

These innovations, or corrections, produced a storm throughout Russia. The patriarch was tampering with the holy books; he was changing the faith of their fathers and undermining the Christian religion. In the eyes of the traditionally conservative Slavs, Nicon had been bought like Judas, and he was likened to the Antichrist. Large numbers of people refused to accept the innovations, calling themselves the Old Believers, and they are still commonly known as the "*Raskolniki*" (apostates).[7] The Raskolniki were very cruelly persecuted by the government, and persecution, as is generally the case, made them even more fanatical. They were hunted down in the forests and massacred, shut up in their churches and put to the flames, tortured, mutilated, imprisoned and exiled, usually to the barren uninhabited wastes of northeastern Russia and Siberia.

The devout and childlike disposition of Czar Alexis had put him under the complete dominance of the awe-inspiring Nicon; and so long as their touching friendship lasted, the stern patriarch could carry his plans of reform roughshod over all opposition. So long as the patriarch retained the devotion of the czar, his army of enemies could not interfere with his sweeping plans. His enmity was with the iniquitous and profligate nobility and the illiterate clergy. The nobles therefore watched for the opportunity to separate the two friends. The animosity of his enemies never relaxed till finally they succeeded in inspiring the czar with jealousy and distrust of the hated patriarch. The unfortunate estrangement between the two once devoted friends culminated in an open rupture in 1658, one year after Paisius Ligarides had received Nicon's invitation.[8]

II *The Fall of Nicon*

Having failed in 1660 to depose and degrade Nicon by a synod of the Russian bishops alone, the court of Moscow was at a loss what to do. The matter remained suspended until Paisius appeared on the scene to help them out of their impasse.[9] Soon after his arrival in Moscow, he was persuaded to join the anti-Nicon faction, but this was inevitable, because the character of Paisius was such (and the wealth was in the hands of this faction) that his enlistment in its ranks was but a matter of time. In vain did Nicon try to find blemishes in the Chiote's character, and in vain did he repeatedly write to the four patriarchs of the East and to the czar himself warning him to beware of the "slippery eel" who had succeeded in gaining the unqualified confidence of Alexis with whom he became a very close friend and confidant, thus assuming the position formerly held by the fallen Russian patriarch. The czar in fact treated Paisius as a "prophet of God." [10] With so much learning at his command, the czar would be able to draw upon the extensive knowledge of his new adviser in his war against Nicon. Paisius now, without shame or restraint, asked for increasingly more money and ecclesiastical robes and gifts from his generous benefactor, who catered to his every request without stint. The renegade archbishop had at last found the proverbial goose that laid the golden egg.

Upon learning of his arrival, Nicon, who was then living in self-imposed exile at the Monastery of New Jerusalem,[11] which he himself had built outside Moscow, sent a representative to extend his welcome and to express the hope that he would do his utmost to reconcile the former friends. Ligarides was pleased with the message and in fact two months later submitted to the czar a memorandum calling upon the monarch to resolve the misunderstanding. "The patriarchal office is the most exalted of all," he wrote, "as a consequence of which everyone agrees that to leave the patriarchal throne unoccupied for four whole years is most absurd. It is something entirely unheard of for the patriarchal church to remain in an eclipse, like the moon, for so long and to be deprived of its lawful shepherd, like a widowed woman, bereft of her husband. One can reason as follows: If Nicon is in fact guilty of crimes, then he should be deposed by synodical decree, since the crime requires punishment, but if he is proven innocent and is guilty of no offence, let him return freely to his seat, so that the confusion may cease. Russia has become the target of derision throughout the world, and all people await the termination of this tragicomedy. Let innocence and justice be bared, for it is whispered abroad that Nicon fled to escape a murderous attack and plot which had been laid for him. Such repute dishonors the entire on grounds of patricide, and all it imputes is a condemnation of Your Majesty; the council and the people are in such deadly sin that the mere thought of it alone is terrible."[12] The bibliophile Paisius goes on to suggest that the Ecumenical Patriarch should be appealed to, and hastens to ask for a favor. "It is known that Your Majesty has collected from various libraries many exceptional books. I respectfully beg you therefore for your permission to have free access to the collection, so that I may inspect and study those Greek codices." It is possible that Paisius found in the collection the precious homilies of the great Photius, which were to create such a ripple of excitement among scholars in subsequent years.[13]

It is not known how Nicon managed to obtain the original copy of this letter of Ligarides to the czar. Nicon, in any event, wrote a lengthy response to Paisius in Slavonic, which was translated into Latin by the teacher Epiphanius Slavenitski, in which the exiled patriarch describes how he had been in complete agreement with the czar for six years, but disagreed with him only concerning the matter of the ecclesiastical court which the state wished to appropriate for itself. He goes on to describe how friction arose between him and the monarch and how the synod, whose validity he denied, condemned him. Then he adds, "You write about the books that were collected by His Majesty from different countries which lie uselessly stored away, but these books were assembled at my order and not at the suggestions of the czar, and they have now been carried away to our distant monasteries. Health be with you, and do not forget to remember us in your prayers."[14]

III *Further Intrigues*

Upon receipt of the communication from the exiled patriarch, Ligarides sent on July 12, 1662, at the command of the czar, a verbose reply which is so indicative both of the bewildering problem involving Nicon and the attitudes that the Chiote assumed. He expresses in the opening his perplexity in being situated between two disputants, Nicon and Alexis, blessed by the one and befriended by the other, and uses an image which he recalls from his sojourn in Rome to describe the dilemma. He compares himself with Augustine standing in the painting by Francesco Francia, the Bolognese artist of the fifteenth century, between the Madonna and the crucified Christ, and saying, "Whither I should turn, I do not know, for from the image of the Madonna I am suckled, and from the lordly crucifixion I am both nourished and refreshed." [15] His Catholic background again emerges to the surface in this passage, for Madonna worship was so indicative of the Latin tradition. The encyclopedic cleric then goes on to relate the story attributed to Theophilus of Alexandria, who, having entered into a dispute between the patriarch and the emperor of Constantinople, had two statues sculptured of the disputants. From the one statue he cut off the right hand as punishment for striking, and from the other he cut out the tongue for insulting. Paisius proceeds after this tale with a further display of his learning by citing a story from Roman history involving Emperor Hadrian. Then he develops his theory on kingship, in which he maintains that the emperor is supreme above all; therefore, Nicon had intruded into alien domain by assuming inadmissible powers. The prelate draws upon further examples, rambling on, page after page, from both ecclesiastical and secular history, no doubt to impress the fallen patriarch. With great subtlety he reproaches Nicon for falling out with the czar. The writer then goes on at great length to develop his theory of kingship and the exalted position of the throne in society, and reminds Nicon of the innumerable favors and the affection that Czar Alexis had showered upon him. Paisius with difficulty attempts to control his deluge of words as he cites Homer, the Arabs, Alcaeus, Pittacus, Archilochus, Hippias, and Aristotle's Constitution of Cyme. Even he feels uneasy about the loquacity, and attempts to justify his "Asiatic prattle." [16]

In a subsequent apology and defense of his career in Russia, the prelate quotes extracts from the letter.

I came to Moscow for my own purposes, of my own free will, without mission or invitation. I came not to dispute with Nicon, nor to judge him, but to seek for alms. Nicon at first wrote to me engaging me to help towards a pacification; and by the order of the Emperor I answered him. In my answer I wrote, "For all thy struggles and sufferings may God repay thee with a worthy reward! But I, finding myself between two parties of combatants, am at a loss to which side to turn." So I might have precluded; but now it is too late. I know that thou lookest to a right purpose and end. Thou criest aloud, "Repent," imitating that other Nicon whose name thou bearest. But the Emperor feeds me, and day by day bestows his graces upon me. Afterwards I was in the habit of conferring with the most splendid synclete respecting certain political affairs; and I did not depart from Moscow quite so soon as Nicon wished, but stayed on there only, as was manifest, to work up the case against him, and to make war on him by innumerable writings. The Emperor is the earthly god; Emperor at once and Bishop, as we say to his praise of Constantine; of a mixed origin, sacerdotal at once and royal, like Aristobulus, who was at once high-priest and king; and to speak briefly, with the single exception of officiating in sacred things, all the other episcopal privileges are clearly represented by the Emperor, and in respect of them he acts lawfully and canonically.

Although trained in Rome where papal authority was deemed supreme over secular authority, Paisius maintains the Byzantine position wherein the Emperor as vice-regent of God can intervene in ecclesiastical affairs, a tradition initiated, of course, by the first Constantine. But this is not surprising.

The Chiote summarizes what we suspect drew him like a magnet to the Emperor's faction.

And I, above all, will shout like a stentor, to proclaim his boundless liberality towards myself. Yes, indeed! Yes, indeed; I do both kiss and embrace the hand which enriches strangers. Yes; yes; I kiss the hand which supplies our outward and inward wants, which bountifully lavishes what exceeds all necessity and want. In truth, O Nicon, thou oughtest not to have been so free spoken, to have represented the truth so plainly, so categorically, to the Emperor and boyars, without being in the least abashed. For if thou hadst behaved more politically, flattering and humoring them, thou wouldest not have come at least to such a condemnation.[17]

The wily archbishop here presents succinctly the formula for what in his mind was the key to survival and advancement: Do not speak the truth so plainly or categorically to superiors; behave cunningly and artfully; flatter and humor. Although this formula worked well for him in the course of his travels, eventually he was to pay the heavy penalty for straying too long on the devious path of deceit. It is true that Nicon paid an equally heavy price for speaking the truth, but in the long run Nicon joined the ranks of the immortal saints, whereas Paisius Ligarides sank into the quagmire of ignominy.

The conciliatory tone of the letter of Paisius indicates that initially at least the anti-Nicon faction centering around the czar sought some kind of compromise to terminate the impasse. When Nicon had been absent two years from Moscow, the czar had called an irregular synod of Russian bishops to sit in judgment on him for having "of his own will abandoned the most exalted primatial throne of Great Russia and so having abandoned his flock and thus having caused confusion and interminable contention." In October, 1660, this so-called synod decreed that by his conduct Nicon had absolutely abdicated and ceased thereby to be patriarch.[18] This decree was rejected by the implacable Nicon who placed the objections to the charges against him in the hand of commissioners sent to interview him in his convent. The hostile boyars[19] were anxious to remove the adamant prelate. Having failed in 1660 to depose and degrade him (and without his absolute degradation his enemies did not think themselves secure), the matter remained suspended until Paisius helped them out of their difficulties.[20]

The boyar Simeon Lucianovich Streshneff, one of the most powerful of Nicon's enemies, had been excommunicated by the patriarch because this noble had called his dog by the name of Nicon, had taught it to sit up on its hind legs and to cross its paws in the offensive form of benediction which Nicon had introduced.[21] Streshneff was instrumental in introducing Paisius to the boyars of the council and through the council to the czar. Alexis consulted him, took his blessing, and not only caused him to be received by the Russian bishops as if he had brought canonical recommendations from the East but even made him their president and spokesman, thus putting the Russian church and clergy as well as himself and his council under the blessing of an unknown stranger.[22]

The paid advocate and conductor of the proceedings for the nobles and the czar was given thirty questions in writing by Streshneff for each of which a reply was requested. These concerned the conduct of Nicon and the duties of a patriarch. On August 15, about a month after the verbose epistle had been addressed to Nicon, Paisius submitted answers to these questions which delineate the specific charges against the unfortunate Nicon by his enemies. The Chiote again had occasion to display his vast learning, and he spares neither wit nor pedantic reasoning in presenting his arguments against the actions of Nicon, which on the surface at least appeared irrefutable. In the prefatory letter accompanying these *Replies of Ligarides* to the *Questions of Streshneff*, he writes:

I am grieved that I do not know your Russian language so as to answer you directly as I would have preferred. When translators encounter a passage they do not understand, they make clothes-pegs of these or interpret the passage in accordance to their own beliefs and wishes churning out their inner ignorance. I therefore entreat you to see that these replies be translated first into the Russian tongue and then into Latin so that I may see in what manner your interpreters have made the translation, since a mighty and great empire has need of such persons who can correctly convey the identical meanings of other tongues in order that it can judge properly what has been said or written with confidence.[23]

We thus discover that Paisius never learned the Russian tongue well enough to write in it. During his sixteen-year sojourn in the country, he wrote all his works in the two languages of which he was a master. It is most probable that he acquired a speaking knowledge of Russian, but he felt at home only in Greek and Latin.

IV *The Interrogation*

It would perhaps not be out of place to cite one or two of the questions submitted to Paisius by Streshneff in writing, and the replies the former submitted to the nobleman:

Question III: Is it proper, once the priest or even the Bishop has donned his robes, to comb his hair at the Holy Altar and to groom himself before a mirror in church? For Nicon was accustomed to doing this before the divine service after he had donned his priestly garments?

Reply: This is highly improper, for it is a womanly habit and unbecoming even to the ordinary mortal, let alone the clergy. . . . It would have been better had he groomed himself in his own cell before entering the church.[24]

Question XXX: Nicon excommunicated the boyar, Simeon Lucianovich, because his dog performed an act of benediction. Now, does this constitute grounds for excommunication?

Reply: When a mouse nibbles into the holy bread, this does not mean that it partakes of communion, since it is not receptive of sanctification. In like manner, when a dog pretends that it is giving a blessing, it is not a blessing, although such pranks should not really be played in a Christian country. They are animals, like the magpie and the parrot which learn to imitate, and they amaze us how well they can do so. The same applies to the elephant and the ape as well as to the faithful dog about whom Aelian[25] writes at length in his work "On the Characteristics of Animals." So, then, the Patriarch should not chastise in such instances, since excommunication does not happen to be something to play about with in a frivolous and base manner, for it is cheapened and degraded to such a degree that the mere thought of mentioning such a thing is shameful. If a Turk ridicules the mysteries, does that mean that the mysteries are to be scorned? Of course not, for the sun is not dirtied in the mud, nor befouled by the mire, but remains unsullied and unspotted as before. Now, what kind of judgment, what kind of retribution is this, that one should be delivered into the hands of Satan, that we be lost eternally, to be divorced from our mother church for unbecoming causes. No, No. The divine is not driven or motivated by absurd impulses. Excommunication and chastisement and divorce from God are befitting only when the sin is mortal.

Blastaris[26] writes in the chapter on excommunication that, "one should not be excommunicated without reasonable cause," and he cites the following: The first is that one is not excommunicated on those grounds specifically excluded by the sacred canons, and the Bishop who excommunicates for a senseless cause is guilty, and cannot chastise because he has flouted the very purpose of the excommunication by debasing it. And so excommunication should be practiced in fixed instances when a sin happens to be committed. Not for every sin, but only for that transgression specified by the canons, and the party to be excommunicated should be summoned and examined first. And if he admits his sin frankly and openly and repents, he should not be ejected from the body of the church. Did Nicon consider the matter and in other serious instances did he fail to do so? [27]

Paisius adds an epilogue to the thirty questions in which he cites a fable of Aesop.

It seems to me that now more than ever the Lord's sermon is true, that saying, "Ye blind guides, which strain at a gnat, and swallow a camel." [28] For Nicon does not see his own huge wooden beam, but looks upon only the wooden chip which he finds in the eye of this or that person. If he looked upon himself, and practiced the "Know thyself," and examined his own person, he would not have done all those things he has so senselessly done, and still does. How well indeed did Aesop put it when he said that every person carries over his shoulder a sack in which the one end contains his own shortcomings, and the other end the faults of others. But the part that contains his own failings are strung behind his shoulder, and the part containing the faults of others is hung before him. The spirit of truth says, "He who has ears to hear, let him hearken," and, "He who is wise let him understand." [29]

Throughout his replies the unabashed Chiote speaks of truth, honesty, and excommunication without constraint, at a time when he had already been excommunicated by the patriarch of Jerusalem. But for the time being, at least, this was unknown in Russia.

The end for which the *Questions of Streshneff* and the *Answers of Ligarides* were written was attained. The answers were translated into Slavonic and read with glee by the foes of Nicon, who had many copies distributed widely throughout the capital. A copy fell into the hands of the defiant patriarch, who soon drafted a lengthy reply in which each of the charges against him was refuted. His voluble reply abounded in quotations from the Holy Scriptures. Nicon had finally realized that his faith in Paisius had been misplaced and that the learned cleric was a formidable enemy. Through people who were well disposed towards him (and several of the boyars were), he made inquiries concerning the Chiote's character and past history. He records:

Some report of him that he is not an Orthodox son of the Holy Eastern Church, but a member of the Western Roman kostel; that he was with the Pope thirty years as a deacon; and he lived among the Moutiani [Wallachians] a long time; and disseminated much Roman heresy. He bade widower priests to marry again; and said that young monks and nuns should marry, and eat meat. And the Metropolitan of Moldavia wrote about him to the Ecumenical Patriarchs, and they anathematized him, and ordered that he should be unfrocked and he went off from Wallachia to Poland; and in Poland he was a long time with the king, and he celebrated [mass] in all the kostels.[30]

V *Further Involvement*

A Greek, and knowing how to deal with the Greeks, Ligarides advised the council and the czar to summon a synod at which the four patriarchs of the Eastern church would be invited to review and judge the case of the fallen patriarch. The czar had already sent copies of the accusations and the replies of Nicon to the ancient sees of Constantinople, Jerusalem, Antioch, and Alexandria. To press the czar into action, Paisius suggested that the letters of appeal should be composed at once and in Greek, inferring of course to himself, so as to have no need of an interpreter. Moreover, this would enable the czar's secrets to be kept the better and the patriarch of Constantinople to be able to give correct judgment in so grave a matter.[31] When the letters were drafted, Ligarides recommended a fellow countryman, the monk Meletius, to deliver them personally. The Chiote Meletius had been in Moscow since 1655 and was well acquainted with the affairs of that city. Together with another Greek, one Stephen, they were also instructed to denounce Nicon verbally to the ecumenical patriarch and to justify those who were anxious to see him condemned. Heavily laden with liberal gifts for the patriarchs, the envoys Stephen and Meletius set out on their mission in the autumn of 1663. At the same time, Paisius wrote to Dionysius, the ecumenical patriarch, assuring him that he was working for Orthodoxy. He also wrote to Nectarius, patriarch of Jerusalem, asking him on behalf of the czar to condemn Nicon.[32] Feeling secure in his intimate relationships with the czar and the council, Paisius wrote to Nectarius as though his excommunication by that patriarch had never taken place. Nectarius could scarcely be ignorant of how Ligarides was honored and employed by Moscow.

In the meantime, the affairs of Ligarides had never prospered more. His intelligence, Jesuit dexterity, and his *savoir-faire* were valuable assets in an uncouth but wealthy environment. His aims were twofold: firstly, to amass a fortune as soon as possible; and secondly, to use the emperor as an intermediary in restoring his position with the eastern church, a position which had been badly shaken by the excommunication pronounced against him. His timely arrival when Nicon's embroilment with the czar and the boyars had reached a feverish pitch could not have been more opportune. The latter needed him desperately, and Paisius joined forces with them to further his personal ambitions. The Greek ingratiated himself with Alexis by using his formula of flattery and adulation, subtlety and polish, which contrasted so much with Nicon's rigidity, formality, intractability, and pretentiousness. Paisius did not waste time in exploiting this friendship and soon submitted a long series of requests to which the generous czar responded unstintingly.[33]

VI *Special Requests*

There exist in the archives of the Bureau of Foreign Affairs in Moscow a number of detailed documents dealing with the activities of Paisius in this particular sector.[34] Soon after his arrival in the Russian capital, the Chiote petitioned the czar to redeem Christian hostages of his diocese who were in the hands of the Turks. He falsely maintained that he had reached an understanding with the Turks by which he was to deposit with them every year the sum of 100 efimki as ransom money. He begged the emperor to provide the money so that "I would not be expelled from my see, and the impious Turk does not convert to Islam the flock of which I am pastor." [35] Alexis responded immediately to this brazen prayer from one who was no longer metropolitan of that see and who had absented himself from his flock for ten years. The covetous prelate was not discomposed in the least in abusing the confidence of the Russian monarch. Evidence indicates that Paisius sent the money intended every year for the ransoming of Christians to his nephews in Chios instead.

In September of the same year (1662), he put in a special request for the maintenance and support of his living quarters. Bewailing the fact that, though the stipend and sustenance allotted him were sufficient for him alone, he could not possibly support his aids, servants, and three horses. The emoluments were soon augmented. Alexis increased his allowance so that the domestics and the "wretched" animals would not starve. A second request immediately followed, and he was provided with his episcopal accouterments, including a chasuble and a miter. Not only did the czar hear his prayers with compassion, but gave him additional gifts such as a caftan, a fur-lined cassock, and a fur-lined coat of double sable. In 1663, the prelate addressed the monarch with a new string of requests, among these one for a carriage and horses with new breeching since the old had rotted. In another plea, he asked that an allowance be given to his deacon Agathangelos. In yet another request that same year the Chiote reminded Alexis that he had come to Moscow to ask for alms, "in order to pay the dues of my diocese accruing to Nectarius, the Patriarch of Jerusalem, and to the Turks; and also to provide for my own sustenance." Then he adds, "I have been residing in Moscow for three years, at the request of the Emperor, and I learn that the patriarch of Jerusalem is very irritated with me for being so long absent from my diocese, and there is no bishop to administer to my flock in my absence, and I have not paid my dues to the patriarch, nor to the Turks. My diocesans borrowed a large sum to meet the necessary debts." [36]

The sum, amounting to 1700 efimki, was given him by the emperor for discharging the fictitious debts. Next, Paisius asked that the alms be provided in gold coin so that he could forward the sums more conveniently in time of need. As a result Alexis ordered that Paisius be given 850 gold pieces in place of the 1,700 efimki. Being moved by the anxious and careworn prelate so concerned about his flock (though he had no flock), over and above these contributions, Alexis showered more gifts on the deceptive Chiote who had so charmed and beguiled him.

These requests were followed by a spate of others. He received a further increase in his allowance and was provided with generous rations of salt, wheat flour, wood, and honey from the palace stores. Paisius, his archimandrite, his archdeacon, his cellarer, and the latter's deacon, were all provided for without stint. The cellarer of the Metropolitan of Nazareth, who was quartered in the Paisius residence, his interpreter, and two domestics, were also supported by the czar; and lastly, as a special favor from the emperor, the same Metropolitan received from the palace fish and caviar, wine and hydromel.[37] In a subsequent prayer, the voracious prelate asked Alexis for a supply of wood and timber. Rather than supplement his maintenance, the czar ordered that he be given an extraordinary grant of one hundred rubles with which to renovate the furnishings of his residence, and he was given special permission to purchase wine from Archangel, duty-free, transportation to be provided by the state.

Somewhat later (in 1666) Paisius solicited from Alexis a daily sustenance for his nephew who had arrived from Chios. He also asked that his obsolete sleigh be replaced by a new one, and that the daily maintenance for himself and for his domestics be increased further. In still another petition in 1667, he asked for a larger daily allowance for both himself and his nephews, and for good measure, for his domestics, "since," he averred, "we are dying from hunger." [38]

The often impertinent demands were always met by the generous monarch. So we find our Chiote living in luxurious fashion at the expense of the state treasury which expended annually the not contemptuous sum of 361 rubles. Paisius could now easily amass a sizeable fortune. If windfalls of 850 gold coins at one stroke happened only occasionally, the prelate nevertheless let no opportunity slip through his fingers, and in time became very affluent. The czar indeed was kindhearted and derived much pleasure in distributing gifts and favors.[39] Both Paisius and his kin in Chios prospered.

Like so many of his countrymen, Paisius could not resist the attractions of commercial enterprise, even though he wore priestly raiments. In a report from the archives of the Alien's Bureau in Moscow, one reads that he had wanted to purchase some valuable sables and have these sent to his diocese. A certain Greek by name of George was dispatched to find these and received from Paisius the sum of two hundred rubles with the promise that he would provide him with the furs. The merchant neither gave him the sables nor returned the money, but Paisius persuaded Alexis to order the merchant either to supply the sables or restore the funds. From this report it is not difficult to deduce that Paisius was not above trafficking in furs. He would purchase these items in Moscow at low cost and, by using his more trustworthy Greek acquaintances as intermediaries, or his nephews, he would have the furs delivered to the markets of Constantinople where they fetched a high price. Utilizing his close association with the czar, he could demand and receive respect from the Greek merchants of Russia whom, we are sure, he would on occasion fleece with the utmost impunity. As in Moscow today, and as in Byzantium many centuries before, all foreigners were under close surveillance, unable to make the slightest move without the permission of the authorities. All foreign merchants required special permits to sell their wares and could buy only those items that were specified by the state. Paisius therefore was a very useful person to know, and by wielding his influence with the palace, he could obtain certain permits and privileges, but of course for a price.

The grand chartophylax, or keeper of the archives and documents of the Patriarchate of Constantinople, was at this time one John Caryophylles, a person of considerable learning and influence, and one of the few friends about whom Paisius could boast. The latter wrote to him in 1663 an elegant and graceful letter in which he again displayed his mastery of Greek and his close friendship for the man.[40] We do not know whether he wrote to Caryophylles on the Nicon affair or whether the deacon Meletius and the envoy Stephen had conveyed his views to the keeper of the archives personally. In any event, Caryophylles was sympathetically disposed to the anti-Nicon faction, although we do know that the majority of the Greeks in Constantinople and the Turkish dominion were for the most part warm supporters of the fallen patriarch.[41] When word had reached the Ottoman capital that the deacon Meletius and Paisius, both Greeks, were fighting Nicon, a storm of hostility arose especially against Paisius whom most recognized as a Latinizer and an impostor. Caryophylles himself was many years later to be defrocked, but as a Calvinizer. In this particular letter to his friend, Paisius first praised Caryophylles for his great learning, then exhibited in delightful turn of phrase and simile his classical learning with such expressions as, "sweeter than Hymettus honey . . . full of ambrosia and nectar . . . by the learned Hermes . . . full of a myriad graces . . . dressed in the beautiful robes of the Muses of Helicon . . . overflowing with the Attic Sirens. . . dancing with Aristotle, Socrates and Plato . . . a new Plotinus, Theophrastus and Themistius." He then abruptly descended from the heights of Parnassus to the more mundane levels of a certain George and the merchants of Moscow.[42]

Nicon in the meantime was pleased with the news that he was to be tried by the patriarchs of the East, but he was not happy that Meletius and Stephen were the envoys, the former of whom he had denounced as untrustworthy. In a desperate move to see the czar personally, he emerged from his monastic retreat to visit Moscow, but his overture was abruptly rejected and the infuriated patriarch according to one report fulminated against the emperor and the royal family, going to the extreme of invoking a curse upon them.

VII *Personal Encounter*

When word reached Moscow of his action, a committee of interrogators was sent to investigate the rumor.[43] Paisius Ligarides was one of the representatives on the committee. This was the first confrontation of the wily Chiote and the dynamic Russian, and the meeting was provocative and explosive. The inquest upon Nicon by an unaccredited Greek stranger was too much for the patriarch. In his *History of the Condemnation of the Patriarch Nicon,* which he wrote four years later (in 1667), Paisius records that when Nicon refused to have anything to do with him unless he could produce canonical letters, he whispered into the ear of Nicon, in Greek, something worse than "stupid clown," an epithet altogether too coarse either to utter aloud or to write.[44] But this incident is probably a fabrication.

Paisius began to speak in Latin, with an interpreter present, and opened the inquiry by asking the Russian why he had cursed the czar and his family. Nicon strove to change the subject, but Ligarides persisted in demanding a direct answer. Denying that he had pronounced a curse on the czar, the enraged patriarch snapped back:

> Thief, unbeliever, dog, self-ordained, peasant! Have you any credentials from the Ecumenical Patriarch? This is not the first time you go about from country to country causing dissensions as you are doing here. . . . Why do you wear a red mantle contrary to the canon law?

The agitated Paisius replied:

> Because I am from the real Jerusalem, where flowed the unadulterated blood of the Savior of the world, and not from the false Jerusalem[45] which is neither new nor old, but a third Jerusalem, that is, of the coming Antichrist.

Nicon then countered with a further question: "Why do you not speak to me in Greek, in your mother tongue, but use the accursed language of the Romans?"

The Chiote retorted that he did not use Greek because the patriarch could not understand such a golden tongue. The heated argument continued in much the same vein, and Nicon refused to converse with Paisius any further after a final outburst against the Chiote:

> O thou new schismatic, or I will say heretic, from the condemned Constitutions of Clement, and from Esop (sic), and from ravens and jackdaws, and from other lying and swinish and accursed books, contrary to Canons lxv and lxxv of the Apostles, and Canon i of the Seventh Ecumenical Council, citest lying testimonies, like a raven thyself going about land and sea making divisions, as thou hast done in the land of Moldavia.[46]

Paisius reported to the czar who smilingly asked: "Well, then, did you finally meet Nicon?"

The prelate replied: "Indeed I did, but better that I had not seen such a monster. Better that I were blind and deaf so as not to hear his cyclopean cries and his thunderous babble."[47] The Chiote's comments were indicative of the acuteness of the affair which had shaken the Russian church to its very foundations.

There survives a description of Nicon by Paisius Ligarides which reflects the fondness of the Greek for the numerous branches of the occult sciences including astrology, dream interpretation, palmistry, and physiognomy. The belief in such sciences was widespread not only among the Greeks but also among all peoples of Europe at the time. Paisius used his knowledge of physiognomy to deduce the character of the Russian from facial features:

> Before I saw the notorious Nicon, I used to study, out of curiosity, a painting of him, and I wanted so much to examine his features even in an illusive icon. When I finally saw his features which had been drawn by my friend John, an exceptionally good German artist, I remained speechless, believing for a moment that I was gazing upon a giant or cyclops, and I deemed those people who were born sightless and were unable to see very fortunate indeed in not being in a position to set eyes upon such a monstrous form. If anyone for example met him suddenly, he would think that he was looking at a ferocious wolf. Regard, for the sake of interest, the head of Nicon. See how massive and bulky it is and without a brain! Notice how black is his beard, like the raven or the boar. Regard the narrowness and the wrinkles of his brow, which are marks of narrow-mindedness and suspicion. . . . The length of his body is indicative of his unreasonableness and absurdity, while the projecting eyebrows reflect his harshness. His eyelashes indicate impudence and babbling talk, his long ears virulence of tongue.[48]

In his *Book of Prophecies,* as we shall see, Paisius devoted entire chapters to the interpretation of magical formulas, oracular sciences, and dreams. He asserted that he was not really convinced by dream interpreters, but incorporated the lore in his work "as a curiosity or for the sake of knowledge." [49] Nevertheless, he dedicated to the czar a treatise on *The Interpretation of Dreams* on the occasion, no doubt, of some misgivings that the czar had when the Patriarch Nicon communicated to him in writing the contents of his remarkable dreams which had made him abandon his monastic retreat and hasten to Moscow.

On the night of December 17, 1664, an extraordinary occurrence took place which brought the deadlock between the exiled patriarch and the palace to a climax. Nicon had received an urgent plea from one of the few boyars who was still friendly with him that he should come to Moscow unannounced on the festival of Peter, the first metropolitan of the city, and invite the czar to join him in the cathedral, as was formerly the custom, and as if nothing had happened to their once great friendship. Meditating on the contents of the letter, Nicon stretched out on his stone bed to rest. While asleep he dreamed that he was again in his beloved cathedral, and he saw arising from their graves the whole line of metropolitans of the see who had preceded him. One by one these hoary prelates arose from the line of tombs stretching around the walls, and took him by the hand and raised him once again to his patriarchal throne. Nicon awoke from his dream and taking it as a sign of divine providence, returned without delay to Moscow that night on the eve of Peter's festival. At dawn he was in the cathedral in his former place standing erect before the patriarchal throne. He invited Alexis to come to the church to receive his blessing.[50]

Indescribable confusion and dismay filled the ranks of the nobles, clergy, and the czar with the sudden appearance of the patriarch. The sleepy nobles were summoned hastily to the palace together with the clergy, Paisius Ligarides among them. It was a matter of life and death to them to prevent the meeting of Alexis and Nicon, and they succeeded in preventing it. An embassy was sent to the cathedral:

> You voluntarily abandoned the patriarchal throne and promised to cease being primate: you departed to live in the monastery, and the

Ecumenical Patriarchs have been informed as much. Why do you now come to Moscow and enter the cathedral without the permission of the Czar and Holy Synod? Return, therefore, to your monastery.[51]

With bitterness in his heart, Nicon obeyed the command and withdrew to his self-imposed exile but only after crying out that he resigned the patriarchal seat, that a new patriarch should be appointed in his place, and therefore there was no need for the synod which had been summoned to try him. Nicon's fall was henceforth inevitable, and his fate now rested with the synod of patriarchs and bishops which would eventually sit in Moscow to condemn him. Nicon's aim to make the church supreme over the state had ended in abject failure. For a brief period, he had shared with Alexis considerable power in civil affairs, for the czar, out of deep respect for the dynamic prelate, initially submitted to this interference. Nicon's reforms in the church were to be accepted by the synod, but his interference in secular matters, together with his personal actions, were condemned. As in Byzantium long before, so in the Russia of the great patriarch, the state had triumphed over the church.

VIII *The Great Synod*

Chagrined by Nicon's abrupt entry into Moscow, Alexis wrote to the patriarchs assailing this latest uncanonical action. In a letter to Nectarius of Jerusalem, he begged the prelate to visit Moscow personally or at least to send a representative.[52] Nectarius, whose sympathies lay with Nicon, knew that those in Moscow were set on deposing Nicon by whatever means necessary, and he declined the invitation. But not anxious to offend the czar, who was after all a primary source of alms for his see, he sent a letter suggesting a compromise to terminate the affair which had so disrupted the peace of the great church.[53] Dionysius of Constantinople pleaded that he could not attend unless the sultan granted him special permission to leave the city, In a most unexpected and surprising letter to the czar delivered by Stephen, he named Paisius Ligarides as his exarch or representative in Moscow for this particular affair:

We have appointed Kyr Paisius, the holy and learned Metropolitan of Gaza, and have sent him faculties, appointing him to be our Vicar, to defend those canonical chapters, and to solve every difficulty and doubt, objected from the other side, and to direct the trial, in conjunction with the holy synod of the local Bishops, presiding in it as representing our persona in that affair to its final settlement.[54]

Paisius had foreseen that Dionysius would not attend the synod, and he laid his plans accordingly, no doubt in conjunction with the special envoy Stephen and with the connivance of John Caryophylles who was cognizant of all the correspondence involving the Nicon affair by virtue of his position in the patriarchate. When Stephen returned to Moscow, Ligarides let it be known that he was appointed by Dionysius to act as his representative.

It appears that the czar accepted the letter delivered by Stephen as genuine, but only because it suited his purpose; in fact, he gave publicity to the contents whereby Paisius was to represent the see of Constantinople at the trial. But, not knowing the results of the mission of Meletius, who was busy in the East persuading the Greek prelates to attend the synod, he sent a monk named Savvas on a secret mission to Dionysius in 1665, then ex-patriarch and metropolitan of Thessalonika, and to Parthenius, the new patriarch, not only to beg them to come to Moscow, but at the same time to inquire into the actions of the envoy Stephen in the Ottoman capital, and whether in fact Paisius had been officially appointed as their representative in the Nicon affair.[55]

Dionysius informed Savvas that:

The Greek Stephen was never received by me: only the chartophylax John Caryophylles spoke to me about writing a letter in which I should say that the Metropolitan of Gaza was to be my exarch: but I gave him no permission for this; and if any such letter has been exhibited by the Czar, those are tares sown by the chartophylax. As for Paisius Ligarides, he is not a scion of the seat of Constantinople, nor do I call him Orthodox: for I hear from many [e.g., Nectarius] that he is a Papist and a bad man. And as for the Greek Stephen, do not let him go either: for he has done great mischief to the Orthodox Church.[56]

Nectarius, too, was approached on the same matter, and he asked the envoy to make it known in Moscow that no one had been appointed patriarchal exarch. The czar kept the special mission secret, but so anxious was he to settle the affair that had dragged on for seven years that he gave free rein to Paisius to help expedite the trial. So it appears from the evidence available that the letters of appointment and recommendation were forgeries drafted with the connivance of John Caryophylles, the only friend Paisius had among the Greeks in the capital, and the envoy Stephen. It is curious, however, that in writing his *History of the Condemnation of Nicon* in 1667, Paisius related as a fact his appointment as patriarchal exarch.

Meletius in the meantime was busy persuading the patriarchs to visit the Russian capital. He succeeded in inducing only those of Antioch and Alexandria, together with some twelve bishops, who made preparations to set out for Moscow. Macarius, patriarch of Antioch, who had made the long and exhausting journey to Russia and the Danubian principalities in the course of which he had met Paisius nine years before, made up his mind to revisit Moscow because, as Paisius records, "of the persuasive argument . . . honeyed discourses . . . and the most sweet eloquence of Meletius." [57]

It is reasonable to assume that most of the letters addressed to the eastern patriarchs by the czar were drafted by Paisius himself. Internal evidence and the style of writing would indicate as much. Paisius suggested that the czar write also to Neophytus, metropolitan of Adrianople, who was one of the few higher prelates sympathetically disposed to the Chiote.[58]

In the midst of the frenzied preparations for convening the most august assembly of divines which Russia was ever to witness, the position of Paisius was shaken, but only momentarily, by the revelations of the deacon Agathangelos. The wily Chiote managed once again to weather the storm unscathed. Agathangelos was once in the service of Paisius when a robbery took place in the residence of the Greek. It appears that Agathangelos was implicated in the theft, together with other domestics of the household, as a consequence of which the deacon was imprisoned. Appealing for a pardon, he was released, whereupon he fled to Nicon's monastic retreat. There he expounded at great length on the crimes of Paisius, and it goes without saying that the fallen patriarch was delighted with the string of accusations brought against his archenemy. Welcoming the new information, he provided the deacon with funds and letters and dispatched him to Constantinople to undo the work of Meletius and Paisius. Unfortunately, however, the deacon Agathangelos was apprehended en route to Kiev by the czar's agents and cast into prison. Nicon's last desperate attempt to turn the tide against his foes had come to nothing.[59]

At about the same time, the czar sent a delegation to Nicon to remind him of those statements he had made whereby he considered the summoning of the patriarchs superfluous, deemed himself no longer patriarch, and suggested that a successor to the Moscow see be elected. The delegation asked Nicon to put these statements in writing. Nicon set out at length the conditions that forced him to withdraw from the patriarchal throne which was to be filled by a new appointee. He was asked on the occasion to allow those criminals condemned to death to be given the last sacraments, but Nicon refused to repeal this or any of his other rulings. The adamant prelate then addressed to the czar a searing attack against Ligarides, listing many accusations based on the evidence supplied to him by Agathangelos.[60]

The strong indictment created a major turbulence in the circles of the czar and boyars, and when the emperor presented him with these charges, Paisius was not at a loss for an answer:

> If even one of these slanderous charges is established, then I shall be guilty of all the others, but, if a single accusation is disproved, I shall then consider myself innocent, because my hierarch of Jerusalem, Saint James, has truly said that he who maintains the whole covenant of the law, but is guilty of one transgression, is guilty of all transgressions.[61]

The prompt rejoinder by the prelate pleased the czar, who at once granted him a small bishopric much to the further chagrin of Nicon. Some days later, Paisius petitioned that the charges against him be examined by the Russian hierarchy even though in accordance with canonical law he should be tried by the patriarch of Jerusalem. And so the czar assembled the clergy to examine the accusations carefully, especially the first two charges against the Chiote; namely, that he was not orthodox and did not adhere to the traditions of the fathers of the church, and that he believed in the magic arts and in astrology. Numerous witnesses testified on behalf of the Chiote, but the deacon Agathangelos, who was dragged before the august assembly in fetters, shouted in an unseemly manner that all his charges against Paisius were indeed factual. If we are to believe the information Paisius gives us,

Agathangelos was unable to substantiate his imputations and was sent into exile for defaming the character of the prelate. In his place of exile, the deacon repented, then confessed that his charges against the archbishop were groundless, upon which Paisius forgave the slanderer.[62] The character of Agathangelos was much like that of Ligarides. He saw eye to eye with Paisius on most matters.

Paisius's latest triumph was absolute. On December 15, 1665, he submitted to the czar a long report, which, unfortunately, survives only as a fragment.

When, at the behest of Your Majesty I visited Nicon with the boyar Prince Nikita, the Metropolitan of Astrakhan and others, he called me an unbeliever and a heathen, and later sent you a document blaspheming me and accusing me as a heretic and an impostor. Now letters have arrived concerning my person which confirm me as the Archbishop of Gaza and as a person of excellent learning and wisdom on which grounds I am appointed as official judge and exarch of the apostolic throne of Constantinople.

There remains now nothing in the way to clearing my reputation and making known my title of Metropolitan so that all the blasphemies uttered by my opponent Nicon may be refuted. And I beg Your Imperial Majesty that the patriarchal letters proving my innocence be divulged to the council, for it was in the presence of the entire synclete that I was disgraced at the instigation of that fiendish devil Agathangelos in whom Nicon and Nicon alone believed. . . . A vagabond and intruding priest he calls me because I have no canonical letters. Even the most holy Patriarch of Jerusalem, in his many letters to you, never made such frenzied claims and never described me to Your Majesty in such words, although he knows that I am not on the side of Nicon. In his letter, Dositheus, the archdeacon of the Patriarch of Jerusalem, does maintain that I am supporting the faction of the boyars and that I handle the imperial correspondence written in your name, and which, apparently, in his opinion at least, contributes to the decadence of the Eastern Church. But he never wrote that I was a heretic and a vagabond without canonical letters. That is the vein in which the archdeacon should have written if it were so, since I do belong to the see of Jerusalem.

I therefore beg you to inform Nicon that on the evidence of the actual letters from Dionysius, I do in fact hold the apostolic throne of Saint Philip, one of the seventy. In any case, Nicon had recognized my priestly title when he wrote to me, but subsequently he scorned me and did not admit that I was a prelate, maintaining as he did that I do not have the letter of ordination. But this letter I do have from the hand of the Patriarch of Jerusalem who tonsured me and ordained me Archbishop in the Church of the Holy Sepulcher of Our Lord. . . .[63]

The tone of the document reflects the growing insecurity of Paisius and betrays a fear that his unsavory past would soon be uncovered by Alexis and the Russian hierarchs. Sensing perhaps that the czar would consult Patriarch Dionysius secretly concerning the validity of those letters appointing him as representative in Moscow, the inventive Chiote ended his report to Alexis by asking that he be given permission to depart:

I, the unworthy one, beseech that you release me, your humble servant, O most divine Emperor, before the local synod convenes, and in nowise do I mean ecumenical, at which the Ecumenical Patriarchs are expected. After all, I really came not to enter the discussions and trials involving Nicon, but only because of the large debt of my episcopal see for which I received your generous alms, half of which were pilfered by Agathangelos. . . . So release me before the assembly of the synod so that I can look after my own soul. Since I have endured so much before the synod meets, what must I suffer after it ends? Enough, most merciful Lord and Master, enough! I can no longer serve your palace, so release me, please release me. Just as I came of my own free will and without invitation, so let me depart willingly and freely for my episcopal see to look after my soul and my God-given flock.[64]

It becomes rather obvious that Ligarides, when writing the memorandum, was convinced that the czar would not release him, for he had become the monarch's right-hand man in the complicated Nicon affair, and his most trusted confidant. Moreover, Alexis considered his presence in the forthcoming synod, which all in Moscow awaited impatiently, as absolutely essential.

As we have seen, the patriarchs of Constantinople and Jerusalem, being sympathetically inclined to Nicon and therefore anxious to avoid entanglement in the affair, used one excuse or another to justify their inability to absent themselves from the Ottoman domain. On the other hand, the mellifluous deacon Meletius had succeeded in persuading the prelates of Alexandria and Antioch to attend the synod in Moscow. Their journey to the Russian capital was long and most arduous. The aged patriarchs traversed the wild terrain of Iberia and moved along the shores of the Caspian Sea to reach Astrakhan, from where they crossed the Volga and proceeded along the western bank of the mighty river to the new fortress town of Simbirsk,[65] then cut across the wintry overland route to reach Moscow finally on November 2, 1666.[66] Two days later they were received by the joyous czar on which occasion Paisius Ligarides delivered an oration of welcome in his usual inimitable style which did not fail to charm the two hierarchs of the eastern church.

So the time at last had come to resolve the impasse which had been rending asunder the very foundations of the Russian church. Nicon had dominated the scene for twenty years and was to fade quickly from the stage immediately after the trial and condemnation; and the church was to return to a relative normalcy which it had not enjoyed for those two decades. The most venerable assembly of divines which Russia has ever witnessed convened for the condemnation of the greatest prelate whom the eastern church had produced in modern times. Present were, besides the two august patriarchs from the East, thirteen metropolitans, nine archbishops, five bishops, thirty-two archimandrites and abbots, eight higher priests, as well as monks, clergy, and the highest in rank of the Russian boyars.[67] The impressive hierarchical gathering, among them resident Greek clergymen of Moscow, met in the hall of Nicon's palace in the Kremlin which he himself had built.

The opening meeting of the synod took place on November 7 over which Czar Alexis, like Constantine the Great at the First Ecumenical Council of Nicaea, presided. All documents relating to the charges against Nicon were presented for scrutiny; two bishops were appointed as translators. At the insistence of the patriarchs, Paisius Ligarides was also selected to explain the case against the Russian prelate. "As from now," the czar said, "you have him at your side, and from him you will learn all the details." [68] Paisius listed the accusations to be considered, and added several further charges for good measure, such as collecting vast sums to establish monasteries, surrendering the ecclesiastical courts to secular authority, and changing the traditionally established practices of the church. The Chiote was in fact to write the *History of the Condemnation of Nicon* the following year, copies of which were translated and distributed widely. The *History* he dedicated to his patron Alexis, who, it appears, was reluctant to accept it, no doubt because of the new accusations brought against the author by the patriarch of Jerusalem. Copies of the Greek text exist in both Russia and Rumania.[69]

Eight meetings of the synod were held to resolve the Nicon affair alone. The second dealt with the legality and nature of the body, to forestall any possible challenge on the part of Nicon as to its sanction. In the course of the third assembly, on November 28, it was decided officially to summon Nicon to appear. The defiant prelate questioned the authority of the patriarchs to try him. A further summons was sent during the fourth synodical council on November 30, at which the two senior prelates verified that they were indeed delegated to represent also the two absent patriarchs, whereupon Nicon at last decided to appear before the solemn body. On December 1, during the fifth session, he appeared for the first time before the seated judges. In front of these, communicating with them through an interpreter, still claiming his rank as patriarch and declining to sit at the appointed place because he could not sit on the patriarchal throne, Nicon stood erect and glared defiantly around the assembly. He discerned many familiar faces, including Macarius of Antioch, the same patriarch who eight years before had seen him in his highest pomp. And for the first time in eight years the czar and the fallen patriarch again stood face to face. The sight of his old and trusted friend standing, and robed as if for a capital sentence, so moved the monarch's heart that he could not contain his tears. To the consternation of the clergy and boyars, Alexis descended from his throne, approached the erect cypresslike prelate, took his hand tenderly, and burst forth into a doleful cry:

> O most holy father, why have you put upon me such a reproach, preparing yourself for the Council as if for death? Do you think for one moment that I have forgotten all your services to me and to my family during the plague, and our former friendship? [70]

The touching exchange between the two former friends spread dismay among the nobles and the clergy. Soon, however, Alexis began to read the accusation against the unbending figure with much compunction broken by sobs that were impossible to repress. The charges were bared one after the other.

At the seventh session of the council on December 5, Nicon was again summoned to appear before the ecclesiastical tribunal. He maintained his proud and defiant bearing to the end. Alexis could not endure being present at his condemnation. The two former friends were never to meet again. It was during the eighth session of the synod that Nicon, still carrying his sarcastic bearing, heard the sentence of his deposition, degradation, and exile. The sentence was pronounced by the patriarch of Alexandria, with his former friend and counselor the patriarch of Antioch standing beside him:[71] "Why do you degrade me without the presence of the czar?," the fallen prelate cried out. Then, with dry irony, he offered the patriarchs a large pearl from the front of his headpiece, which they had removed with their own hands from his head: "It will help to support you under your oppressions in Turkey, but it will not last you long. Better stay at home there than go wandering about the world as mendicants."

IX *Triumph and Defeat*

After being stripped of his patriarchal trappings, he was sent under armed guard for keeping until the next day when the prisoner was led into exile. The greatest prelate that Russia had ever known was to spend fifteen years in isolated confinement. Ten years after the trial, in 1676, Alexis lay on his deathbed. Messengers were sent once more to Nicon to grant the emperor forgiveness. The forgiveness was sent verbally, but Alexis was already dead. When the news reached the broken Nicon in his solitary cell he groaned aloud: "The will of God be done! What though he never saw me to make our farewell peace here, we shall meet and be judged together at the terrible coming of Christ." [72]

Nicon was also to outlive Paisius Ligarides by three years. The new czar, Theodore, son of Alexis, set the now aged and unbowed warrior at liberty, and allowed him to return to his beloved monastery of New Jerusalem which he had built with Alexis; but he died on the journey there on August 17, 1681. Thus ended one of the most brilliant yet unhappy chapters in Russian ecclesiastical history in which the vagabond Chiote played such a prominent part. But Paisius was to atone eventually for his infamous role at the trial.

The synod continued to meet until as late as June 1667, and it recognized and set the seal to all the reforms introduced by Nicon. The Old Believers were condemned, and the reformed and rejuvenated Russian church again found its bearings. The important ecclesiastical rulings introduced by Nicon remained forever monuments to that synod in which for the last time the Greek church, through the presence of its hierarchy, helped to shape the final form of the great church of Russia.[73] The synod was in effect a victory for Nicon's policy of imposing Greek practices on the Russian church. On the other hand, it was a defeat for Nicon and his attempt to place the patriarch above the czar. The Byzantine tradition had again been victorious.

Paisius Ligarides seemed to have triumphed. The *History of the Condemnation of Nicon* was written for his personal glorification and for that of the czar to whom it was dedicated.[74] The wily Chiote had emerged from the trial as one of the czar's most trusted confidants in church affairs. And it goes without saying that Paisius used his position to the fullest to enrich himself further.

The crowing prelate's position in Moscow was firmly entrenched with the deposition of Nicon. The vacant patriarchal throne of Moscow could now be filled by the aged Joasaph in whose appointment the two patriarchs of the East together with Paisius had a hand. Paisius, in fact, entertained the hope (as he had in the Jerusalem see) that in the event of a new vacancy, which because of the advanced age of Joasaph would not be too long, he might himself be raised to the exalted throne for his many services to the czar. But his hopes were too flighty, and soon his position was to deteriorate. The blow was struck by Nectarius, the patriarch of Jerusalem, who in a letter to the czar received in Moscow on July 29, 1668, declared that his predecessor of Jerusalem had defrocked Ligarides when the latter was still in the Danubian principalities even before he had departed for Russia.[75] Nectarius denounced the Chiote as a Latin heretic and suggested that the czar keep him under close surveillance in case he leave the country and hasten to his old master the pope, and so divulge the secrets of the czar's empire. He added that when he had assumed the throne of Jerusalem (in 1661), Ligarides did not present himself, as was proper, and did not carry patriarchal letters of recommendation for the trip to Russia; that he had abandoned his see uncanonically for fourteen years; that the funds and alms he had collected, from the czar, ostensibly for his see, were sent to Chios; and finally, that with the Orthodox he pretended to be Orthodox, and with the Latins a Catholic. Hence, Paisius Ligarides was neither an archbishop nor a priest nor a shepherd nor a teacher.[76]

The condemnatory letter unmasking and excommunicating Paisius and, even worse, accusing him of Romanizing, should have made some impression on the czar and his circle, but they refused to acknowledge the shameful conduct of the very person on whom the entire Nicon affair hinged. Paisius himself could argue in his defense and persuade the czar that the accusations and charges against his person were undoubtedly made by the friends and supporters of Nicon; furthermore, that his condemnation would be at the same time a condemnation of all the actions taken against Nicon. Indebted to Ligarides for his prime role in the Nicon affair, the czar decided to write to the patriarch of Jerusalem asking him to absolve and to restore Paisius to his see.

In the meantime, however, Nectarius had resigned, and Dositheus Notaras was elected patriarch of Jerusalem.[77] The new patriarch wrote and confirmed that Ligarides had been originally degraded and anathematized by his predecessor Nectarius, not for Romanizing, but for crimes which modesty could not allow him to name; moreover that Paisius had shown no signs of penitence for his transgressions. But to please the czar, since he had asked for it, and since Paisius had been useful to the czar by getting him out of the difficulty with Nicon, Dositheus would treat the Chiote's vices and sins as virtues. He added ironically that by way of honor and praise for these actions he would enclose a letter of absolution.[78] Thus Alexis succeeded in having Ligarides absolved, though the latter must have felt that his influential position with the emperor was somewhat shaken. It is curious that the still unrepenting and arrogant Chiote had written to his friend John Caryophylles, when he learned that the young Dositheus was elected to fill the vacant chair of Jerusalem (he himself probably entertained the hope of obtaining this patriarchal title), that, "there not being available a man in Jerusalem, Deborah ruled." In the letter of absolution accompanying the letter to the czar (October 1669), Dositheus wrote that "out of consideration for the Czar's request we hold Ligarides absolved and blessed of God Almighty and of our Lord Jesus Christ, and restore him to communion, and allow him to be entitled Bishop of the see of Gaza." And he added, "Moreover, we had recommended to our father Nectarius and to all the synod, to absolve him in like manner as he by the grace of the Holy Ghost is absolved by us out of affection for the most autocratic Christian Czar." [79] At the same time he wrote to Ligarides chastising him for his many thoughtless actions, and pointed out that he absolved him only for the sake of the czar; furthermore, that should he in any way commit another offense, of any nature whatsoever, the intervention of his imperial patron would in no way ever again be of avail.[80]

Of the letters addressed to the czar, Paisius was handed only the letter of absolution so that he could use it as he saw fit for restoring the status which he had lost through the action of Nectarius. But new problems arose for the Chiote. Many of the clergy in Moscow refused to recognize the validity of absolution given by Dositheus. The Russian patriarch himself objected to this on grounds of incompleteness and ambiguity. Since Paisius was defrocked by Nectarius, his successor Dositheus had no right to absolve him in accordance with canonical law. Using the ever-ready logic and rhetoric, Paisius refuted the claims of those who maintained this argument in a petition to Alexis, but we detect an insecurity in the once overconfident prelate. Ligarides no longer pretended innocence, but only pleaded that the absolution obtained from Dositheus was valid and sufficient, and prayed that a revision of the unfavorable judgment by the Russian bishops be made.[81] From that time on the position of Ligarides in Moscow deteriorated more and more until the final blow was struck by Dositheus himself, who, upon hearing of new charges concerning the conduct of the Chiote in the Russian capital, excommunicated him in April, 1671, finally and irrevocably.[82]

Alexis would not dare to appeal again directly to Dositheus. However, since it was in his interest that Paisius retain his ecclesiastical title, he addressed on August 14, 1671, a letter to the Greek governor of Wallachia, one John Doukas, to intercede with the patriarch of Jerusalem on behalf of Paisius. But Doukas would not hear of any absolution for the former archbishop of Gaza, for the Chiote's ill reputation had traveled far and wide. It is curious that despite his excommunication, Paisius continued to use his ecclesiastical title as archbishop, as evidenced in a letter he wrote on October 27, 1671, to a certain monk Theodoret, concerning the exegesis of a passage from the Apocalypse on Gog and Magog.[83] This letter again shows the prelate's wide range of learning.

X *The Man of Letters*

During his residence of ten years in Moscow, however much his reputation as a personality may have suffered, his reputation as a man of letters did not. Paisius had on many occasions met distinguished foreign visitors and diplomats in the capital, and these never failed to be impressed by the man's wide learning. The Austrian ambassador to the Russian court,[84] for instance, considered him to be the most cultured person in the whole of Russia at the time.[85] The Swedish envoy John Lilienthal provides further impressions of the Chiote and also supplies the information (for whatever it is worth) that Paisius had studied both in Rome and Padua, from which latter university he received a doctorate.[86] Paisius had met the Dutch plenipotentiary and scholar Nicholas Heinsius as a result of which the most exciting discovery to Photian scholars came to light. The Chiote's knowledge of ancient ecclesiastical literature and sources, and his love for rare books, were well known. Heinsius received from Paisius a list of sermons of the great Byzantine patriarch Photius of which some were, until that time, unknown to scholars. Among these sermons or homilies were two remarkable ones which Photius had delivered on the occasion of the two attacks against Constantinople by the "Ros" (the Russians).[87] This was the earliest reference to Russia to come down to us, and Paisius had the manuscript in his own possession; but how he acquired it we do not know. Heinsius had hoped to obtain the copy with the view to having it published in the West. Protracted negotiations were held with Paisius to that end, but various obstacles intervened. All foreigners in Moscow were kept under police surveillance, and the Russian authorities forbade further meetings between the Dutchman and the Greek. As the former wrote after returning to his country:

> Once I invited to visit me the Metropolitan of Gaza, Paisius Ligarides, a Greek, very well educated, inasmuch as he had passed the best years of his life at Rome, an extremely polite old gentlemen.[88] But the next day, by direction of Athanasius Nashchokin, who has the superintendence of all relations with foreigners, I was given to understand that it did not please them at the court that I, without asking permission of the Czar's majesty, had invited to come and see me a man who stood so high among the clergy. A like message was also sent to Paisius,

for having complied with my invitation. So we were both shut off from further communications. Meanwhile I saw nobody who would have been better able than he would have been, by his conversation, to make me closely acquainted with Russian affairs.[89]

Heinsius left Moscow in August, 1670, but he had received from Paisius some extracts from the Photian homilies together with their titles. On his return to Stockholm, the Dutch scholar and poet allowed the matter to lapse, although he had received from Ligarides a further reminder, in March, 1671, in which the Chiote hinted that some interested parties were willing to pay him as much as one thousand gold pieces for the manuscript of Photius.[90] The opportunist Chiote lost no occasion to try to enrich his coffers.

The position of Ligarides in Moscow had deteriorated so rapidly that he thought it wise to abandon the city in which his reputation had become so stained. He therefore announced his intention of visiting Palestine, though whether he was serious about such a destination is highly improbable. Paisius was given official permission on May 4, 1672, to leave the Russian capital, but it was not until the following year, on February 13, that he finally set out on the journey.[91] He was provided with a retinue and funds for the trip; he was allotted a pension; and at the same time he asked that his residence, books, and other possessions in the Simonovsky monastery be put in the care of the dragoman Nicholaos Spatharius.

Upon reaching Kiev, Paisius abandoned any idea of continuing his journey farther. It is most likely that he had received bad tidings from the East; even Panayiotis Nicousios, the grand dragoman of the porte, had thought him too dangerous for the peace of the Orthodox church and forbade his entry into Ottoman territory. The now unsure and isolated Chiote lingered on in Kiev. In the meantime, the authorities of that city had received directives from the czar to keep a close surveillance of his every move, not to allow him to leave Kiev, and to intercept his correspondence. The atmosphere in the old Russian capital of Orthodoxy had become ever more oppressive and confining. Paisius was not allowed to preach; he wrote to the emperor in November, 1675, that the political and church authorities of the city had become most uncooperative; also, that the patriarch Dositheus still would not relent and give him absolution. To occupy himself, Paisius turned to lecturing on philosophy at the academy and these lectures were delivered in the Latin tongue. He also composed several theological tracts in the Orthodox spirit against the Roman church. It may well be that the aged former prelate had now finally returned to the church of his forefathers. Several of his last letters reflect such sentiments. Surprisingly, however, in this final stage of writing, even in his correspondence with the czar, Ligarides used Latin as his vehicle.

The governor of the province was ordered suddenly by the emperor to send the unhappy old man back to Moscow. Alexis refused to receive the degraded prelate and treated the now forlorn Greek who had served him so loyally and efficiently in the Nicon affair with unprecedented frigidity. His former circle of friends in the capital also completely shunned him. But with the death of Alexis, and Theodore's assumption of the throne, Paisius had hoped that perhaps his lot would improve; this hope, however, was short-lived. In 1676 he appealed for permission to leave for the East once more. This was granted him, but Paisius again proceeded no further than Kiev. The despondent and crestfallen man of letters died there soon after, on August 24, 1678, and was buried by the command of Czar Theodore in the monastery of the Brotherhood. All his possessions were turned over to that monastery.[92]

Thus ignominiously the once promising career of the unfortunate Paisius Ligarides was terminated, of the man who was one of the outstanding clerics of his time, but one who, had he chosen a more honorable path, may well have greatly influenced the course of events in the history of the eastern Orthodox church which had such need of intellectuals and learned prelates in the seventeenth century. Had he not become so intricately involved in the Nicon affair, it is quite possible that he would have been the foremost Greek historian of that century, and many of his works would have seen the light of day. But the path he had chosen, his unethical character and unsavory reputation, had set the seal on all he had written. He is remembered today chiefly as the objectionable and selfish author of the *History of the Condemnation of Nicon,* written for self-glorification, and as the man who had once possessed the precious homilies of Photius in his private collection. His greatest work by far, the *Book of Prophecies,* continues to remain unpublished and lies neglected in a dust-laden corner of the patriarchal library of Jerusalem.[93]

XI *Friends, Foes, and Countrymen*

It is difficult to conceive of an individual who could live happily without friends; people normally hunger for companionship. And it is equally difficult to deny that a friend can be and often is an important influence on the growth and development of character. Yet, in the turbulent career of Paisius, spanning more than half a century in such varied countries as Italy, the Ottoman Empire, and Russia, we must look long and hard to single out among the many hundreds of acquaintances whom the Chiote had occasion to make in his extensive travels, a person who could be described as a loyal and lifelong friend. Indeed, the character of Paisius was such that it would be surprising to find even one or two. It is not easy for an opportunist, a flatterer, a backbiter, or rascal to make a friend. Paisius was all these and more.

Certainly, the unique and only enduring friendship was with Leo Allatius who more than any other was responsible for shaping the Chiote's character and career. Paisius looked upon Allatius as his protector, mentor, and exemplar. It is conceivable that, had his mentor not existed, Paisius may well have made the break with Rome final shortly after his return to the East and would have embraced Orthodoxy without further ado. Like his protégé, Allatius was a Chiote who had studied at the Greek College of Saint Athanasius from which he was graduated in 1610, about the time Paisius was born. He was the most learned of the Greeks and one of the better known authors of the seventeenth century who did so much to revive an interest in classical and Byzantine scholarship. Appointed to many posts, he was sent in 1622 by Pope Gregory to Heidelberg to bring back the famous Palatine collection which Maximilian, elector of Bavaria, had donated to the pope. Allatius returned the following year with one hundred ninety-six cases of precious books and manuscripts that enriched Rome's great libraries even further.[94] A mortal foe of the Orthodox church, most of the important works of this prolific writer consist of attacks on that church and the "heretical" Greeks. Allatius died in 1669, the very year in which Paisius began to lose his most favored position in the Russian capital in the wake of the triumphant condemnation and exile of Nicon.

Indicative of the strong bonds that linked Ligarides to his mentor is the considerable correspondence between them which has survived. The wide traveler wrote faithfully to Allatius in Rome from nearly every country he visited, including their native island. From the Danubian principalities there is preserved a letter in which Paisius describes a miracle performed by a Catholic priest.[95] A Russian (Orthodox) priest, so the story goes, had been called upon to absolve a man who had died under the excommunication of the church, as a consequence of which the body had been found undissolved in the grave. Try as he could by various "heretical" incantations, the Orthodox clergyman failed to dissolve the corpse, whereupon the Catholic priest began his ministrations over the dead body. Scarcely had he ended his prayer in which he invoked the pope of Rome as father and teacher of all Christians and the vicar of Christ on earth, when lo and behold the corpse miraculously dissolved into dust. Paisius here writes what Allatius wished to read, and the protégé throughout his mentor's life never once hinted that he had been flirting with the "heretical" eastern church. Allatius died believing that Paisius remained to the last a devout disciple of the Papacy.

The year in which Allatius died, Paisius wrote to his other steadfast friend, one of the only two friends of long standing in the East, the learned John Caryophylles, keeper of the archives and documents in the patriarchate of Constantinople.[96] The Chiote here makes mention of a mutual student they had, and from this can be deduced that Paisius had met Caryophylles in Constantinople when he first visited the Ottoman capital on his proselytizing mission to the East.[97] The bonds linking these two were on the intellectual plane for Caryophylles was in his own right one of the most learned Greeks of the century who had held high office in the patriarchate. He eventually attained the exalted rank of the Grand Logothete, which office he retained until as late as 1691 when he was defrocked as a Calvinizer. His most important work is the *Ephemerides,* an invaluable diary of political events covering a period for which there is a dearth of sources and which now lies in the British Museum Library.[98] Caryophylles was one of the few Greeks in Constantinople who had supported Paisius and the anti-Nicon faction in Moscow.

It goes without saying that the many acquaintances Ligarides had in such distantly separated cities as Jerusalem where the famous Russian traveler Arsenij Souchanov befriended him, and Moscow where the nobility and the czar himself were on intimate terms with him, were but passing encounters. In the eyes of the latter, friendship with the learned prelate was a means to an end, and once Nicon had been condemned and removed from the scene, the Russians had little further use for a person of such character. When, in his last years, Paisius was desperately alone and in need of support, even the czar who had formerly showered such innumerable and generous gifts upon him, turned away in disgust from the fallen prelate.

A Greek, as a rule, has a strong attachment for his birthplace whether this is a mountain village or an island. When he travels abroad, as so many do, he usually seeks in foreign lands his own villager or islander for companionship. Paisius was no exception to this rule. We discover that whether in Rome or Constantinople or Moscow, it was his fellow islanders whom he sought out for companionship. And we can be sure that the only people who were sincerely befriended by him and derived any benefits from the wealth and the influence that the wily Chiote had obtained in the course of his many peregrinations were the close members of his family who lived in Chios and those whose origins were from the same island.

CHAPTER 6

Works

THE Greek author, whether historian, theologian or poet, has four rich streams of tradition from which he may draw for inspiration and guidance: the classical, the ecclesiastical, the Byzantine, which is but a blending of the two with an Asiatic veneer, and lastly, the folklore which links them all. Every postclassical writer, from the early centuries of the great fathers of the church to the most recent poet or novelist, has dipped deeply into one or into a confluence of two or more of these ever-flowing streams of thought. The descent of Greek literature and lore from the Byzantine era to modern Greece was a process in which the broad stream that was already beginning to narrow down soon after the fall of Constantinople was distributed into several smaller and very shallow channels. Throughout the entire Turkish period the nearly dried-up streams barely trickled through to such outlying regions as Crete, the Ionian Islands, and a few isolated pockets of the Ottoman Empire. On the Greek mainland, in the islands and in the mountain fastnesses, the only uninterrupted rivulet was that of the folk song and the folk legend that managed somehow to thrive and to grow through the darkest period in the history of the Greek race to attain a poetic and dramatic form that compared favorably with its European counterparts.

I *The Trickling Stream*

At the time that Paisius Ligarides was studying in Italy, Galileo was imprisoned by Pope Urban for his revolutionary beliefs. John Locke had already formulated his philosophy when Paisius was in the East, Milton dominated English letters, both Racine and Molière had become established dramatists, and La Fontaine had published his collection of fables. Amid its wars, Europe was in the throes of a creativity the likes of which was rarely to be seen again. The Greek world, on the other hand, was going through a phase of transition, instability, and confusion under the Ottoman yoke, torn asunder by conflicting impulses which it found difficult to resolve. The specter of a language which had substituted a popular form for the old system of grammatical forms handicapped the literary activity of its thinkers. The language problem, that bane of the Greek nation, was destined to remain unsolved even well into the twentieth century, at least in the nonliterary world.

If the Greeks were to emerge from the conditions in which they were kept by their political oppressors, the greatest single instrument to attain this was popular education, which, however, was impossible so long as the learned wrote in an artificial language drawn from the springs of a classical and a Byzantine tradition. Under the influence of this national necessity, books began to emerge from the very few Greek presses that existed and these were printed in the popular dialect. Theological works especially and translations of the classical authors into Romaic or modern Greek began to appear, much in the way that Chaucer is modernized for the reader today. The Greek church, partly through liturgical formularies and partly through the intimate relationships between the priesthood and the people, supplied a perpetual link between the spoken Greek and the archaic or stilted idiom of Byzantine prose. It was in such a setting that Paisius lived and wrote.

In examining the surviving works of Paisius, we are immediately struck by the diversity of his learning. Hs did not draw from any one or two of the four streams of Greek thought, but from all four. Imbued with those classical and ecclesiastical traditions (both western and eastern), which he had acquired for the most part in Rome in the early formative years, his restless and insatiable craving for more learning carried him far into the intricate byways of Byzantium and eventually into the rich folklore tradition, particularly that tradition involving prognostication and the occult sciences.

Scholars generally admit that there was no break throughout the long history of Byzantine literature, that there was a continuity from ancient times, and that this ceased abruptly with the capture of Constantinople in 1453, after which it was supposed that a Greek hardly ever put pen to paper except for an occasional grammar, a dictionary, or a translation, until the eve of the Greek

War of Independence. Yet, the long period from the downfall to the nineteenth century constitutes a fascinating period for the study of the language that can be traced, however sinuously, in an uninterrupted descent from Homer to our day. Wherever Romaic or Greek was spoken, the art of literature never quite perished, although admittedly the traces were for the most part faint and the beauty was rare. Nevertheless, for a thorough study of the language, even the minor authors (and most of them were minor) must not be overlooked. It was not until recently that scholars have turned their attention to the publication of obscure works that carry on the literary tradition from Byzantium to modern Greece. The works of Paisius Ligarides fall into this category, for most of them as yet remain unpublished.

Unscrupulous though he was, shallow in many respects, he nevertheless showed a passion for learning which gave him force amid all his meanderings. He may have been pedantic, yet he was fresh and lively, seeking out new paths of learning. Paisius loved the classics, both Greek and Latin, and much in the Byzantine manner he re-created the classical forms for his own world. At times overbearingly pompous, he never lost an opportunity to vaunt his learning. He was a master of the rhetorical art and was extremely fond of subtleties, word play, and paradoxes. Although he protested that belief in the supernatural was a sign of ignorance, he still succumbed to the weaknesses of his fellow Greeks, or for that matter of most Europeans at the time, and wished to believe in the manifold manifestations of the occult sciences. He was always on the defensive by protesting his Orthodoxy in the East and maintaining his Catholicity to his Latin acquaintances in the West. Perhaps his only weakness (ignoring his unsavory character for the moment) is that he was too diffuse and too much a polymath to become the outstanding historian or theologian or grammarian of his century. He wrote in a large variety of forms, primarily on religious matters, but his historical narrative makes pleasant and easy reading. He quoted extensively from historical sources but rephrased the text in the popular form of the language of his day, much in the tradition of the Greek chronicler. Indeed, the works of Paisius constitute one of the primary sources, though unpublished, for the study of the Greek language of the seventeenth century, for the oracular traditions of the Greek people, and for the history of the eastern Orthodox church in general.

His multifarious works, which mark him out as a man of wide culture, recalling vaguely such learned ancestors as Photius or Psellus, can be divided essentially into secular or profane and religious prose. It is true that he tried his hand at poetry, and there have survived several epigrams, that genre of literature to which the Hellenistic and Byzantine Greeks were so addicted, together with encomia in iambic verse to his teacher Petros Arcudius and to Pope Urban. But the verse is highly imitative and artificial, much in the Byzantine style.

II *Homilies*

As an ecclesiastic it is understandable that the greater mass of the works of Paisius should be of a religious content. The surviving manuscripts in both Greek and Latin, which languages he manipulated with equal facility, include sermons on the primacy of the pope, on the procession of the Holy Ghost from the Father, various liturgical tracts, exhortations to the Lutherans and Calvinists, and instructions for the feast of the Holy Virgin. There are extant also several collections of replies which he drafted to questions of a theological nature put to him by the Russians (including Czar Alexis) and the Swedish plenipotentiary to Moscow Lilienthal.

There exists in the library of the University of Athens an autograph manuscript of the Chiote containing eleven homilies of the original cycle of twelve which are very representative of both his style and language.[1] These homilies or sermons are introduced by the author in the usual vaunting manner in the form of a preamble addressed to his patron at the time, the patriarch of Jerusalem. Though secretly a Catholic, the homilies contain no indication or hint of the fact with perhaps the exception of certain passages wherein he is carried to extremes by deifying the Madonna, a practice typically Latin. The twelve sermons of the original cycle represent the twelve feast days (for which he uses as a simile the signs of the zodiac) of the Orthodox church and include the Annunciation of the Virgin, the Nativity of Christ, the Festival of Circumcision, the Purification, the Epiphany, the Transfiguration of Christ, the Four Days of Lazarus (the Resurrection), Palm Sunday, the Passion of Our Savior Jesus Christ, Holy Easter, On the Doubting Thomas, and the Dormitian of the Virgin, the last of which does not survive.

In the ninth homily on the Passion of Christ, Paisius introduces a curious eyewitness account of the Church of the Resurrection. It calls to mind the Byzantine "Ecphrasis" of Paul the Silentiary who described in hexameters the Church of the Holy Wisdom in the sixth century. Its interest to the modern reader and scholar lies in the architectural delineation of the great church of Jerusalem which was subsequently destroyed by fire and rebuilt many years later:

Three hundred and eighteen years after the birth of Christ as this God-trodden land lay deserted, abandoned and trampled upon, the Lord and the most Christian and serene Emperor Constantine, that same monarch who had transferred the scepter of empire to the new Rome, the new Rome which he had built in honor of the Lord and of Mary the Mother of God and which he named Constantinople, did send his mother Helen of blessed memory to the holy city of Jerusalem with incalculable treasure and with unbelievable disposition for the purpose of rebuilding and renovating this God-trodden holy land. The pious queen made much haste, yet took great pains, and with unwavering diligence built and adorned the God-containing sepulcher of the primary life-giving Lord Jesus Christ. No other church in the entire world appears more magnificent or more hallowed. The art of the rhetorician could not possibly suffice to depict it, nor could a historian find words to describe it, nor could any arithmetical power define its figures. I shall attempt to convey to you in a brief and rather cursory manner a description of its most remarkable parts for the enlightenment of those who have never laid eyes upon such a renowned miracle or who have not had the means to look upon it.

This famous temple is situated near the dwellings of the divine David wherein it is reputed the seer king composed his most prophetic psalms. From there and in an easterly direction within bowshot one beholds the vast temple of the Resurrection of Christ on a very high summit. This edifice soars above the center of the site with its two huge domes and a campanile that is extremely large and very tall, the three, I suspect, signifying the three natures of the Holy Trinity. The one dome is covered in lead and joined by cypress planks underneath, thus forming a broad open space measuring about thirty-three feet across, the number signifying the years of our Savior on this earth, and it is sheltered by a wire netting stretching across to keep out airborne fowl. Beneath this dome is situated the most holy and hallowed tomb of Christ together with the twenty-four prophets depicted in mosaic, Saint Constantine and the divine Helena, as well as the august Annunciation adorned in most exquisite mosaic. In this cupola are seventeen arches and eight columns together with ten supporting pedestals, and round about to left and right are the places for the catechumens, and among these columns there are an additional thirteen pillars, seventeen arches and six pedestals.

The Holy Sepulcher itself possesses a beautiful cupola in which can be descried nine arches and ten columns, and superimposed on this cupola is seen another very exquisite dome supported by twelve porphyry columns crowned by gold-inlaid capitals, and this, too, is covered in lead. Round about are suspended eighteen tapers together with a chandelier. On passing through the entrance to the dome on the western side for a distance of about eight feet you encounter the rock upon which sat the angel who asked the unguent bearers why they were seeking the Crucified Christ when he was no longer there but had arisen. The rock is sunk in the earth, but it can be discerned protruding above the ground for about half a span.[2]

The learned cleric then conducts the listeners on a well-guided tour to the tomb of Christ, the four patriarchal thrones, the Holy Table, the sanctuary, then on to the second dome. He cites the interesting fact that of the sixty-five churches of Jerusalem, only eighteen were still in use at the time (in 1652). The prose flows clearly and effortlessly and Paisius manages to avoid the stilted conventions and the obscurity of the Byzantine style; as a consequence, he makes easy reading. We shall have occasion to return to his narrative powers in the section dealing with his masterpiece the *Book of Prophecies*.

III *Epistles*

The dividing line between the sermon and the letter is very hard to discern. When there was no congregation or audience at hand, the ecclesiastic would revert to scriptural exegeses and doctrinal pronouncements in the form of the epistolary art which has a tradition that compares favorably with most forms of literature. Thucydides and Plato helped to establish the tradition in pagan times and Cicero's political epistles set the standard for many centuries to follow. Saint Paul and the fathers of the church helped to establish the Christian tradition, and the endless stream of letter writing flowed through the long centuries of the Byzantine era with its rich production and continued unabated into modern times to culminate in the highly developed epistolary art of the eighteenth century. In the final analysis, letter writing was a form of written speech and it was the easiest way of displaying one's mastery of the rhetorician's art. Since rhetorical proficiency was one of the paths to ecclesiastical eminence, Paisius very wisely cultivated this art in the Greek College of Rome where the fine precision of Jesuit argument was to become a formidable weapon in his hands. He took great pride in his epistolary performance, and we note in the numerous extant letters extending through a period of over thirty years a continual improvement and a more deliberately cultivated form of letter writing. We can trace the gradual mastery of this form from the simple informative (and always tendentious) letters written in the early period of his life to the pious and hortatory missives in his middle and late period.

Paisius was strongly influenced by such masters of the art as Cicero and Photius who had established the standards for letter writing, respectively, in the West and the East.[3] Indeed, the Chiote was a great admirer of the latter and had much to do with the revival of Photian studies in the seventeenth century by virtue of his possession of a unique manuscript containing some of the more important homilies of Byzantium's foremost patriarch. So elaborate had the epistolary art become that letters could be variously classified by subject matter, style, or purpose. There were letters didactic, vituperative, allegorical, ironic, historical, and so on. There survives a short letter by the Chiote to Dragitsanos Cantakuzene in which he displays in a light and frivolous manner his remarkable mastery of the language. The letter contains no more than about 120 words of which over half either begin with the letter "chi" or contain it.

Very close to the epistle in form is the proem, prelude, preamble, or prefatory dedication, commonly encountered in Byzantine literature. This literary form was highly cultivated by Paisius, and perhaps one of the finest such preambles is that prefacing his masterpiece the *Book of Prophecies* which was composed in 1656. In fact, this is the most elaborate preface in Greek literature of the seventeenth, or for that matter, of the post-Byzantine period. It opens with the prefatory dedication to the Czar Alexis calling upon him to redeem the enslaved Greeks. This is followed by an introduction to the reader, then by three proems and finally by three prologues.[4] The dedication to Alexis reads as follows:

Before the most devout Emperor Heraclius had set out on his campaign against the great king of the Persians Chosroes who had captured so many thousands of prisoners and had plundered numerous fortresses, he had a dexterous artist paint a beautiful drawing embossed in silver which portrait he carried in his bosom as a treasure. When he marched out on his campaign and reached the Turk River, from which the Turk derives his name, he encountered there the ruler and commander of the Agars[5] to whom he showed this beautiful portrait of his daughter. Heraclius promised to give her to him as wife if he helped in his war against the Persians. This was, in the eyes of prudent men and the far-seeing holy fathers, an ill-omened augury, for, they said, that he had promised not his daughter as much as willy-nilly the very Roman Empire itself.

And now, Your Most Serene and Mighty Majesty Alexis, like another Zeuxis,[6] I, too, have gathered together, as he did from amongst the Sicilian girls of Acragas, the most beautiful to make a single composite portrait of Helen, from various books throughout the world all that has been said and reputed about renowned Constantinople, from which you received both your faith and kinship directly through your forebears from Sophie Paleologue, daughter of Prince Thomas.

And thus, Your Highness, to all the wretched Greeks everywhere you have become with God their only hope, and in accordance with the titles of the image recently made of you, "the salvation of Greece, the defender of the faith." There is no need to go too deeply into the significance of names and their derivations for a start, but Alexis in the Greek tongue does signify "assistant," deriving from the verb "alexo" which means "help." It may be that divine providence has granted you such a name, thus faintly presaging and foretelling that you shall assist and help our race to fulfill the prophecy of Saint Andrew, the Fool for Christ's Sake,[7] who mentions the Russians by name as our liberators, as does Methodius of Patara. Even Matthew Bessarab, upon hearing that the great monarch Alexis had led his troops into battle personally, and that Zenobius, the Hetman of the Cossacks, had paid obeisance to him, and when he learned of the many fortresses he had taken from the Poles, cried out, "I know now that such great moves on the part of Alexis are incited by none other than the Lord Himself." [8]

There comes to my mind the words of the late Metrophanes, Patriarch of Alexandria,[9] who told me personally that whoever lives another sixty years will see many and unexpected things. Cyril, Patriarch of Constantinople,[10] ascertained that he had read somewhere that a king of the Agars whose name begins with an "M" would destroy Constantinople, just as Mohammed whose name begins with an "M" did capture it, in much the same way that a Constantine built and Constantine Paleologue lost it. Martin Crusius[11] also records some Turkish oracle which predicts that 200 years after that famous empire of the Romans was captured, the sword of the Christians would be unsheathed and the Turks would be driven out from all lands. And in accordance with the figures, Constantinople was taken by Sultan Mohammed in 1453; and now the year is 1656, so that 200 years have already passed and there are two additional years in which we hold you victorious and triumphant. Not only because you have taken Smolensk and Lithuania, but have routed the Tartars, the wing of the Turk, and you have terrorized the entire Black Sea region with your 32 ships. What if you were to cross the Danube and enter the Danubian provinces? In that event the famous prophecy would be fulfilled. Moreover, it rests in the hands of the Lord. May you, to use the words of Pindar, have a long life and attain deep old age with prosperity and tranquillity and be untroubled and free of every sorrow and evil. Amen, Amen, Amen.

Your devoted well-wisher
and humble servant.

IV *History*

The Greeks have at all times excelled in the writing of history. Indeed, no nation, with perhaps the single exception of the Chinese, has had such a vast corpus of historical literature or a longer uninterrupted tradition beginning with Hellanicus and Herodotus and terminating with the four historians of the downfall, a full sweep of two thousand years. Generation after generation of historians could not ignore the fact that they were the heirs of a great past and as a result there existed a continuity and no break with the classical world such as occurred in western Europe in the Dark Ages. The Greek had a strongly inculcated sense of the flow of history; whether he was a retired citizen of means, an emperor, a civil servant, monk, or theologian, he felt strongly the need to maintain the tradition and to record the events, as had his many ancestors before him. Such a phenomenon was not to be observed in any of the nations of the West that could boast some semblance of a reasonably long history. And historiography was maintained among the Greeks on a high plane until the Ottomans destroyed their national existence in 1453. Nevertheless, even after the disastrous occurrence, the chronicle tradition somehow continued to thrive.

Histories can be divided, generally speaking, into two clearly defined categories: history proper which was inspired by the writers of classical Greece, on the one hand, and the chronicles which became the popular kind of history writing until even after the fall of Constantinople. While the former was intended primarily for the cultivated and intelligent reader, the popular chronicle was written for the layman and the masses. Whereas the historian felt compelled to write basically on contemporary events, the chronicler would write a universal history (thus reflecting the ecumenical idea of one empire and one church) beginning with the Creation and concluding with his own times.

The Byzantine historians wrote conscientiously, using the works of Herodotus, Thucydides, and Polybius as their models. The chroniclers, on the other hand, whether monkish or laymen, would begin with the Old Testament story and compile their histories with sources extracted from previous chroniclers. Since the audience consisted for the most part of monks and simple folk, all odd bits of information that such an audience wished to hear were included and these were animal fantasies, miracles, astronomical phenomena, earthquakes, plagues, and the like. A striking characteristic of the chronicle was the fondness for detailed description of the personal features of their heroes, however factual or imaginary. Unlike history proper, the chronicle was that kind of written record which spread rapidly to the West and to the eastern peoples of the Byzantine Empire where they enjoyed tremendous popularity. Hence, despite their admixture of fact and fancy, they have become more important (and oftentimes the only sources) for a proper study of the civilization of the Middle Ages and for the post-Byzantine centuries. Moreover, these popular chronicles served their purpose well by providing some kind of intellectual stimulation for the common man who would otherwise have had very little entertainment.

In the century in which Paisius lived several popular chronicles were produced in a simple, flowing style in which the language was an odd agglomeration of the spoken dialect interspersed with learned elements. By far the strongest influence was that of the Biblical tradition, but the body of the work was of necessity in the demotic or spoken tongue. One such chronicle contains elements of Roman, Byzantine, and Turkish history up to the reign of Sultan Murat IV (1623–40). But the most read of all chronicles in the seventeenth century was the so-called *Chronographia* of Dorotheos of Monemvasia, which begins with the creation of the world and terminates in the year 1629. This was first published in Venice in 1631 but was reprinted in many subsequent editions. Paisius, in fact, had access to this work.

Like all learned Greeks, unable to resist the affinity with history writing, the Chiote produced four works of which, however, only two survive and a third, *A History of the Patriarchs of Jerusalem* written in 1652, was incorporated by the patriarch of Jerusalem Dositheus in his own history. Dositheus admits that he owes much to the learned cleric's work, which consisted of eighty-three folios. He adds that the history of the patriarchs was carried up to the time of Heraclius; moreover, that two sections of the book were devoted to attacks on the eastern church and particularly against the great Photius and in defense of the primacy of the pope. The history was subsequently anathematized by Nectarius, patriarch of Jerusalem, and Paisius was defrocked as a consequence.[12]

His first history was that of his beloved birthplace. This *History of the Island of Chios* was mentioned by his mentor Leo Allatius and praised highly by him, but the work has not survived.[13] In his *Book of Prophecies,* Paisius cites the history in several passages and refers to it as the "Chian Chiliads," no doubt under the influence of the *Chiliads* of Tzetzes.

The best known of his historical works is in fact a defense of the role he played in Moscow, the *History of the Condemnation of the Patriarch Nicon.* Written for self-glorification it was dedicated to his patron the Czar Alexis in 1667. Alexis, however, declined to accept the dedication. The manuscript, which was never published, had a curious story of its own, for it was carried by devious routes to Cairo from where it was eventually brought back to Moscow and it now rests there. The original work consisted of three books.[14]

The fourth and by far the most outstanding work is not strictly a history, although the greatest bulk of the *Book of Prophecies* is historical in content. In recording and interpreting the oracular ejaculations of such prophets as Daniel, Andrew, Methodius of Patara, and other apocryphal writers on "events past, present and future," Paisius draws upon the long line of both historians and chroniclers of Byzantium. He rephrases in the popular idiom of the day entire passages from such unlikely bedfellows as Zosimus, Tzetzes, Scylitzes, Codinus, Manasses, Gregoras, Cedrenus, Eusebius, Sozomen, and Eutropius. He had access also to a vast range of Western authorities and many contemporary works which he cites profusely. The manuscript of this hitherto unpublished collection of prophecies was completed when he was yet in the Danubian principalities in 1654 and was dedicated to Alexis two years later. The unbelievably wide scope of his reading and sources can best be gauged by citing but a few passages at this stage of the voluminous work consisting of no less than two hundred seventy-one closely written folios. For instance, we note that, when discussing Russia, he uses as his source the Primary Chronicle, a copy of which he may have seen in Rome or in the Danubian regions.[15] Again he takes the occasion to call upon the Russians for liberation against the Turks:

> The monarchy in Moscow is traditional and is descended from us Greeks, and therefore as a true successor is closely related and should by right take over the empire of the Greeks and free us from the most barbarous tyranny which has enveloped and dominated us today.

In an interesting passage wherein he gives his own interpretation of an oracular enunciation concerning Crete, he writes:

> But I think this prophecy refers to the present war in Crete which Sultan Ibrahim started because of the seizure of his eunuch and the gifts which he was sending to Mecca.[16] In 1644 he dispatched an armada, making believe that it was intended to attack Malta, but in fact was destined for unhappy Crete. When it sailed past the Cape of Thodorou, the Capitan Pasha[17] entered Canea and after twenty-two days the city capitulated and the inhabitants surrendered. But much starvation occurred and many men were slain, so many in fact that the oracle was fulfilled. . . . But the Sphakiotes, those excellent bowmen, have not yet been completely subdued. And we keep hoping that powerful fleets will soon come to liberate their suffering land. And especially if the Europeans come, just in the way that the Venetians yearly arrive off the coast with a powerful armada and blockade the Turkish fleet and shut the Turks up in their fortresses to their great shame and disgrace. . . . And that is why I say that the oracle really refers to the Europeans and the Venetians.[18]

The *Book of Prophecies* was incorporated a few years later in Moscow by the learned Greco-Rumanian scholar Nicholaos Spatharius in his own *Collection of Prophecies,* a lengthy theological and mystical commentary on the visions of Daniel written at the behest of Czar Alexis in 1673. Thus, even after the fall of Constantinople, the Slavic peoples of the Balkans and Russia continued to turn to the works of Greek authors as primary sources from which they drew for their early literary inspiration and growth.

CHAPTER 7

The Oracular Tradition

DIVINATION has been practiced widely in all cultures but nowhere more so than in Greece. And not surprisingly, all the chief kinds of ancient divination are to be found surviving even to this day in one form or another among the Greeks. In a nation that possesses such an unparalleled historical heritage, it would be surprising indeed if it were otherwise, for history is intimately associated with the art of divination. When peoples are deeply involved in the fluctuations of historical circumstance, the desire to obtain knowledge of hidden or future events by means of supernatural devices is an inevitable sequel. The belief in and desire for close and frequent communication with the powers above become more intense. History and divination walked arm in arm through the twenty-seven hundred years separating Homer in the ninth century before the Christian era and the prophet "Agathangelos" in the eighteenth century of our era. The impulse to gain knowledge of things unseen and things to come was deeply rooted in the character of the Greek; especially in times of national disaster or adversity did this impulse become even more poignant.

I *By Way of Introduction*

The age of Paisius was one such period. Seldom before or after had the fortunes of the Greeks reached such a low ebb. And inevitably this was the period in which they turned more desperately to the channels of divine revelation for some sign of hope for future salvation and improvement of their lot. As in so many instances with established pagan or heathen practices, the church did not repudiate the old ideas of communication with the powers above but incorporated and confirmed these by biblical authority. No pagan practice was more difficult to eradicate than the belief that the movements of the stars in the heavens influenced the lives of men and that the fate of the individual, or for that matter entire nations, could be predicted by those who were versed in their combinations. It was inevitable that the inextinguishable desire to penetrate the secrets of the future should sooner or later develop into various forms of superstition within the Christian church. The loss of faith in the efficacy of the ancient oracles forced men into the more mysterious arts by which the secrets of the future were to be unveiled. And Christendom failed to repress these mysterious arts. Consequently, there grew a vast corpus of literature of prophecy, astrology, numerology, chiromancy or palmistry, and oneiromancy or dream interpretation.

Astrology continued and continues to enjoy a wide popularity even in those societies in which learning was most advanced and divination and superstition were generally frowned upon. In the Greek-speaking world and in the Slavic nations, the form of divination which enjoyed by far the widest popularity throughout a turbulent history was the art of dream interpretation. The degree of importance universally attached to dreams both in antiquity and in modern times is all too familiar to require more than a passing comment. Books on dream interpretation are still eagerly sought and consulted in Greece. In isolated homes in the mountains or on the islands where the Bible never found its way, one may well find a tattered copy of a dream interpreter which is highly respected and frequently consulted. The church has not failed to exploit this firmly rooted belief in dreams as a spontaneous revelation of the divine will especially for the discovery of some miraculous icon of which a large number are to be found in Greece and the Balkan countries.

The fall of Constantinople, the "city of cities," symbol of church and empire, did not in the final analysis generate in the conscience of the Greeks the impressions of an end, but of a beginning, of a period of tribulations which they would have to undergo before the final resurrection and recovery of the empire. In accordance with the fundamental psychology inherent in the Jewish prophecies, grandeur and exaltation contain the germ of decadence, and haughtiness the seed of destruction. Accordingly, now that the fall had taken place, now that Constantinople lay prostrate amid its ruins, the promise of salvation took firm root. Long before the conquest of Constantinople, numerous ominous forebodings predicting the fall circulated, but these assumed an optimistic tone soon after the terrible event had occurred. Then, as always, human nature being what it is, in destruction and adversity a new psychology was born and nurtured wherein people turned to the unknown mystical and supernatural powers for messages of promise. In the early years of the Ottoman conquest prophecies were already profusely circulated among the Greeks foretelling the "end of the kingdom of Ismael." [1] Numerous manuscripts of the fifteenth, sixteenth, and seventeenth centuries containing predictions of future events were read and widely distributed. Even the Ottomans were to some extent influenced by this widespread lore, and many of them believed that they were destined to lose control of the empire after a certain number of years had passed.[2] Many of these prophetic utterances spread to western Europe where the temperament was receptive to the arts of prognostication. And prophetic literature soon took root there to produce among others such famous seers as Nostradamus. But nowhere more than in the Greek-speaking world was such a copious mass of oracular literature produced.

II *Divination*

Scarcely a folio of the voluminous *Book of Prophecies* does not contain some allusion or reference to the prophetic and magical arts, whether these be a supernatural or more naturalistic attempt to explain and to interpret events past, present, and future. In fact, the forms of prophecy and superstition commonly existing among the Greeks from time immemorial appeared to have attained an unprecedented universality and acceptance in the age of Paisius. The modes of divination thrived as never before. Alongside the long-established pagan and Christian modes of prognostication, there grew the more supernatural devices of augury known to special prophets, wizards, or witches. The latter existed in the Greek-speaking world of the East, but nowhere to the extent found in western Europe where the sympathetic Merlin had long assumed a prominent place in the corpus of western literature and where witchcraft had attained its greatest popularity in the fifteenth, sixteenth, and seventeenth centuries to reach its apogee in the infamous witch trials.

However, the western form of witch hunting never reached eastern Europe and the Balkans. One who displayed magical powers, whether priest or old village hag, was esteemed and feared rather than persecuted or punished. The climate of Europe had become most suitable for the cultivation of all forms of divination and magic in both East and West, and Paisius provides an explanation for this. With his customary fondness for the Homeric simile, he describes the depressing conditions of the world in which he lives, conditions in many respects recalling our own age with an altogether too familiar ring.[3]

Physicians have five portentous signs indicating the imminency of the death of their ailing patient. First, when the humors are completely mixed in an unbalanced fashion; second, when the principal limbs are injured or impaired; third, when the stomach can no longer retain food; fourth, when the patient pulls and tugs his apparel to himself; and fifth, when the body turns cold. And these five portentous signs are now very apparent in the condition of the world today. The humor and elements are completely intermixed, for now nations have taken up arms against one another, and kingdoms have risen against kingdoms. How many wars and how many conflicts now beset our unfortunate times! The main limbs of the world body are damaged, and high priests are dishonored, and the churchmen at odds amongst themselves, and hostile one to the other! The world can no longer retain food in its stomach. By this I mean to say that the word of God is no longer effectual because man now attends church through sheer force of habit alone and listens to the sermon only out of curiosity. He pulls and tugs his wearing apparel only to himself, for each person desires to appropriate and to pilfer the possessions of others, though they belong to the church and be dedicated or consecrated to God. And lastly, the entire world body has turned cold, for love has been extinguished. Piety and respect have gone to the winds. The time of which the Apostle foretold in his first and second epistles to Timothy has now come to pass: "Now the Spirit speaketh expressly, that in the latter times some shall depart from the faith, giving heed to seducing spirits, and doctrines of devils; speaking lies in hypocrisy; having their conscience seared with a hot iron; forbidding to marry, and commanding to abstain from meats, which God hath created to be received with thanksgiving of them which believe and know the truth. This know also, that in the last days perilous times shall come. For men shall be lovers of their selves, covetous, boasters, proud, blasphemers, disobedient to parents, unthankful, unholy; without natural affection, truce-breakers, false accusers, incontinent, fierce, despisers of those that are good; traitors, heady, high-minded, lovers of pleasures more than lovers of God; having a form of godliness, but denying the power thereof." [4]

It would be reasonable to expect that as a clergyman of such high intellectual attainment Paisius would frown upon the less sophisticated modes of divination, such as inspection of the entrails or shoulder blades of sheep, observations of the flights and habits of birds (particularly the eagle, the raven, and the owl), chance meetings on the road, palmistry, weather phenomena, and the like. And yet he deals with each of these and more, indicating at least that he was well acquainted with the varied kinds of prognostication that were so widely practiced by his countrymen and was familiar with their many superstitions. We know, for example, that his mentor Leo Allatius, the first Greek folklorist, had written at length on those peculiar goblins known as the "*kallikantzari*" who supposedly emerge from the bowels of the earth once a year and roam freely through the Greek countryside causing havoc and injury to the unwary.[5] It is safe to assume that Paisius, like his mentor, could write with authority on such folklore motifs.

The Chiote goes to great lengths to describe the various forms of the prophetic arts in the prolegomena on divination.[6] He again displays his knowledge of the vast number of authorities on the subject, whether these authors were pagan, Byzantine, or contemporary.

The ancients and the curious sought many and varied ways of foretelling the future. The Phrygians for example were accustomed to consult the flights of birds as a method of divination according to whether the fowl flew ahead or behind, or to the right or left, from which they could divine whether this thing or that was fated to happen. Livy records that the Roman king Tullius did not have much faith in augury and that the seer chastised him severely for not practicing the Roman manner of divination in order that he could rule the better by knowing the future course of events. . . . Telegonus writes on the portentous arts and describes soothsaying by flights of birds as well as a method of interpretation of various trivial incidents in the house known as domestic divination, for example, when a cat or a snake enters the dwelling, or the oil is spilled over, or the wine, or honey; or ashes or a leaf leap out of the fire, or the wood makes a crackling sound or some other such chance incident which would be a portent of this thing or that destined to take place. Xenocrates wrote on this form of domestic divination. Chance meetings on the road were also indications of future events. Some silly fellows would say that if you met some one holding a cabbage or an onion certain things would happen to you. Polles wrote on this form of augury.

Drawing by lots is still very popular today. Dionysius of Syracuse chanced to draw the letter "M" whereupon some one who happened to be present said in jest that he would eventually become a moron (since the word begins with an "M"). But Dionysius wittily retorted by saying "Not a moron but a monarch." Libanius's power of divination by cocks was highly respected as was Iamblichus who laid out in a pattern with kernels of wheat the twenty-four letters of the alphabet which the cock proceeded to eat, and according to the letter he first devoured the seer straightway would interpret the future. There was the case of the Emperor Valens, for example. When the cock began to eat the letter "theta," the foolish man ordered that all people whose name began with a "theta" should be slain.

Today most people use chiromancy by which some specialists predict the life expectancy and the appointed lot by saying that the tree of life begins at the bottom end of the palm in the life-line. And this line branches out into other lines. If the two branches are uninterrupted and of equal length and extend to the second finger, the person will undergo serious illness. But, if it extends to the first or largest finger then it indicates much misfortune. If there be numerous creases over against the large finger it signifies long life. Again, if from the center of the palm the line runs between the fingers, that is, between the second and the third fingers, then happiness is in store. When it is divided here and there it is rootless and the person's destiny is cut. You should know that such lines or creases in the palm indicate also the location of moles on the body. On this Aelian writes at great length, showing what the future of one reads and what he will undergo. At the same time the more learned seers can interpret the future by the creases or folds in the swaddling clothes of infants. Helenus discusses this method of chiromancy.

Another form of chiromancy is that involving twitching movements of the right or left eye, or a part of the body or shoulder, the buzzing or humming in one's ears, or an itch on the foot, about which Posidonius wrote.[7] Moreover, Polemon composed a work on physiognomy wherein he describes the role played by the various members of the body and the categories of these parts. The sophist Adamantinus compiled another physiognomy for the Emperor Constantius. There exists also a genealogical tree in the name of the Emperor Heraclius, as well as a dream book in poetical form composed by Tarasius, the Patriarch of Constantinople.

But nowadays, people put much faith in dreams from which they decipher the course of future events.

III *Oneiromancy*

Paisius then proceeds with oneiromancy or dream interpretation, citing one example after another. He maintains that dreams are not always proven false. On the contrary, many come true, especially those that are sent by divine providence, as when the angel appeared in the dream of Joseph. This is followed by an elaborate dream interpreter, supposedly composed by Tarasius. This long composition containing one hundred ninety-two verses (one of which is missing, probably through an oversight of the copyist monk Baba Yani) has some literary merit. The lines are arranged in alphabetical order in clusters of eight beginning with the first letter of the alphabet and ending with omega. Between the verses, some of which are in rather obscure language or difficult to translate, Paisius inserts an interpretation in the popular Greek of his day:

> Grapes when you eat, the rain will stop.
> Veal when you eat, a sign of sorrow.
> Laughter in sleep denotes much woe.
> A fall in the sea gives you sorrow.
> Olives when eaten denote a good year.
> Lettuce when eaten means future illness.
> Black horses in sleep is a bad omen.
> A monkey in your arms means love for a woman.
> Dead oxen in sleep means hunger ahead.

The learned prelate closes his first prolegomenon by explaining his feelings on the efficacy of dreams and dream interpretation:

> Thus did the old writers treat of dreams which information I insert as a curiosity or for the sake of knowledge, and not because I believe in dreams. . . . Nor do I believe those dream interpreters who teach that if you see a dream on the first day of the new moon, it is a happy omen. . . .[8]

Despite his apparent disbelief in the efficacy of dreams as omens of future events, Paisius nevertheless cites many examples throughout the *Book of Prophecies* which would indicate that he is not being altogether sincere with the reader. Since the Greek church had not repudiated the long-established pagan superstitions, Paisius was not in any way being unchristian by continuing to give significance to dreams as a general means of communion with God, for the belief in dreams as a channel of divine revelation was both firmly rooted and widely spread. The Greeks anciently believed and continued to believe that a dream is a special communication to them from heaven.

IV *Astrology*

No element of paganism was more difficult to eradicate than the belief that the stars in their courses influenced the lives of men. Those prophets who studied the combinations of the heavenly bodies might foretell the destinies of both men and nations. The Scriptures had taught that the astrologer was the child of the devil since he substituted the idea of destiny for that of the providence of God. Nevertheless, astrology enjoyed an unprecedented popularity in the fifteenth, sixteenth, and seventeenth centuries despite the new theories of Copernicus and Kepler. Closely allied to astrology was numerology and arithmetic interpretation. For instance, the astronomical element could hardly be ignored when computing the thorny problem of dating the Passover and Easter. And we discover that the significance of numbers had made a lasting impression on Paisius. He was as deeply versed in mathematics as were his learned peers of the time. Numerology is a recurring theme in his *Book of Prophecies,* and we can assume that he was acquainted with Dante's number mysticism, for instance, and the Augustinian belief in the structure of the world based on the trinitarian three and multiples of that number. With his Jesuit training, Paisius was well grounded in all the sciences and had, furthermore, a complete grasp of the theology of Thomas Aquinas, although he found occasion to attack the philosophy of Aristotle on several counts.

Weather wisdom was still another mode of divination which has survived to this day among the Greeks and indeed among many peoples of the world. Among the former, the God of Christendom is hardly distinguishable from the Zeus of Homer, for both are cloud gatherers and produce thunder and rain. Floods, earthquakes, storms, plagues, and famine are all phenomenal signs sent by the powers above.

Two kinds of divination appear to be commonly believed by people today as contained in the "Brontologium" [Thunder Book] and the "Seismologium" [Earthquake Book] from which are deduced the course of future events. And thus, in the manner in which I described dream interpretation, so now will I proceed for the sake of knowledge with earthquakes and thunder and how the ancients dealt with these.[9]

There follows a citation of a poem in hexameters from the mythical Orpheus or Hermes Trismegistus[10] with the cryptic text. As in the case of dream interpretations, Paisius inserts his version of the obscure language of the "Earthquake Book," which curiously enough is accompanied by drawings of the signs of the zodiac for the twelve months:

When the Sun crosses the Ram, the Ram receives the Sun on March 21. If the earthquake occurs at night, there will be much disturbance and noise in the citadels and men will rebel, and many areas will become deserted. And in the East there will be many illnesses. The marine animals will multiply greatly in number in both sea and river. But if the tremor takes place during the day, oxen, horses, and all four-footed animals will be destroyed. But the fruits of the trees will increase and become abundant.

The "Earthquake Book" is followed by the "Thunder Book," which again is divided into sections of twelve, representing the twelve months of the year.

In March, if it thunders in the Ram, great withering will occur in the East. And there will be much turmoil and loss of life. If this is accompanied by an earthquake then there will be famine. On the other hand, if there is a thunderstorm during the new month, that is to say, during the first phase of the new moon, then there will be a good crop of wheat, of wine and of olives. But if it thunders when the moon wanes there will be destruction and pestilence. If the moon is reddish in color, there will be disturbances and rebellion of the enemy. And if a star falls to earth the ruler of that land will be destroyed. If a rainbow appears, wars are meant and if this is followed by an earthquake then a movement to war is indicated.[11]

Paisius does not give much credence to these modes of divination and superstitious beliefs and proceeds to deride those who believe in such arts of prognostication. As a good Christian he maintains that it is the will of God and that alone which causes thunder and sends lightning and earthquakes to the earth, just as his compatriots believed that thunder was the result of God shoeing His horse or rolling His wine casks, or one of the saints driving his chariot across the heavens. As a thinker, Paisius could hardly fail to recognize that these explanations for thunder and earthquakes were but pagan survivals in Christian garb.[12]

The common folk, as much as Paisius, called themselves Christians and their priesthood was a Christian priesthood. They worshiped in Christian churches and made the sign of the cross at every turn, and the names of God, of Christ, and of the Virgin, were forever on their lips. But with all the external Christianity, they were as pagan and as polytheistic and as superstitious in their souls as were their ancestors. The taking of auspices, the consultation of oracles, and the numerous forms of prognostication continued to survive intact to his day. Paisius, like his fellow Greeks, was intrinsically a pagan in Christian garb.

CHAPTER 8

The Byzantine Heritage

A large part of the great mass of oracular literature that circulated in the Middle Ages and during the Ottoman occupation in the Greek East concerned the fate of the Byzantine Empire in general and of its capital in particular.[1] There were also collections of prophecies dealing with certain areas only of the Byzantine state or of some city or island. For instance, a book of prophecies in the form of a "vision" concerning the fate of the important market town of Serres in what is now Greek Macedonia has survived. More numerous are those oracular predictions dealing with the fate of Crete,[2] to which Paisius devotes an extensive passage, of Cyprus, of Hydra, and of other Greek islands. There are scores of manuscripts scattered throughout the libraries and monasteries of Europe and the Middle East containing oracles that are attributed to such a medley of authors as the Prophet Daniel, a certain monk by the same name, John Chrysostom, Saint Andrew "The Fool for Christ's Sake," Methodius of Patara, Leo the Wise, a certain Leontius, Patriarch Tarasius, and "Agathangelos" among others. Many of these oracles were translated into the Latin and the Slavic languages at an early date.

I *Prophecies*

The prophecies were cast in either prose or in poetic form, usually in the Byzantine twelve-syllable verse, of which the oldest are in iambic trimeters, and these were often accompanied by allegorical or symbolical pictures. The later oracles in the spoken or popular verse, generally much longer, were composed in unrimed trochaic meters of eight syllables.

The great hodgepodge of prophecies can be divided, for convenience, into certain categories or groups in accordance with reputed authorship. For a better and more thorough understanding of the oracular tradition, Byzantine divination should be studied in conjunction with the ancient oracles since we have constant references to Sybilline auguries, the priestess of Delphi, and so on. To these pagan names must be added those of the ancient philosophers and writers whose reputations as wise men had survived in the Byzantine and post-Byzantine periods, such as Chilon, Solon, Aristotle, Plato, Plutarch, and others to whom apocryphal sayings were attributed.[3] But generally, the so-called authors of Byzantine and later oracles can be put into four main groups:[4]

(1) Authors of the Old and New Testaments, especially the Prophet Daniel, whose visions and apocryphal sayings make him the greatest single source shaping the popular legends of events to come. Daniel's prophecies also enjoyed wide popularity among the Slavic peoples. A certain monk by the name of Daniel who lived in the eighteenth century appears to have incorporated much of the prophecies of his biblical namesake into his own prognostic text.

(2) Those oracles referring to the empire or parts of the empire and attributed to the early saints and fathers of the church, such as Hippolytus of Rome, Gregory the Theologian, and John Chrysostom, to all of whom Paisius devotes much space in his *Book of Prophecies*. An entire cycle of visions and prophecies circulating in the East, West, and North on the "destruction of the Saracens" and "the last days" were attributed to Bishop Methodius of Patara,[5] a saint of the fourth century. He is occasionally referred to as an early interpreter of oracles living in the ninth century. Then there is the popular Andrew, "The Fool for Christ's Sake," who predicts the fall of Constantinople and its recovery. Saint Andrew enjoyed a high reputation among the Slavs.

(3) Those Byzantine and later oracles referring to the fate of the empire or parts of it attributed to certain patriarchs of whom Tarasius (ninth century) is one of the better known. There exists a copy of a pseudo-Tarasian codex dating from the nineteenth century on Mount Sinai containing prophecies and predictions on the recovery of Constantinople. One pseudo-Tarasian prophecy deals with the fate of the island of Hydra. Of the successors of Tarasius, the most famous by far as an interpreter of the enigmatic oracles was Gennadius Scholarius, the first patriarch of the enslaved Orthodox church who was installed on the throne by Mohammed the Conqueror.

Both Leo Allatius[6] and Paisius Ligarides refer to his great learning and to his ability in interpreting the difficult oracular texts. Paisius quotes Gennadius at great length and describes him as "the very wise and learned Patriarch Gennadius who lived at the time of John Paleologue and was present at the Florentine Synod. But when he made this interpretation of the prophecy he was yet a layman and a critic of the Emperor's views. And after the bitter capture, he became Patriarch of Constantinople." [7] Paisius also cites a moving monody in prose or lament of Constantinople reputedly composed by the same patriarch which recalls very strikingly the style of John Chrysostom in his oration against the fallen patriarch, Eutropius.[8]

(4) Byzantine and later oracles and prophecies attributed to certain emperors or members of the palace.[9] In 1596, for example, a collection of prophecies appeared in Constantinople which was attributed to the Roman emperor Severus of the second century A.D. Oracles in the name of the great Persian King of Kings, Chosroes, and interpretations of prophecies by Constantine Lascaris, secretary of the palace and not the emperor of the same name, also exist. Compilers of oracles would generally attribute these to more ancient and earlier Byzantine ecclesiastics or wise men to lend age, credence, and authority to the prophecies.

But of all the oracles attributed to certain emperors by far the most famous were those in the name of Leo the Wise, the "most wise," the "most philosophic." The great number of manuscripts circulating especially in the sixteenth and seventeenth centuries indicates that the oracles of Leo were greatly in demand not only in the Ottoman East, but in the West where the threat of further Turkish advances was causing considerable alarm.[10] The oracles in his name are in both the learned, or obscurantist, language, and in the popular demotic vernacular. There arises a considerable confusion in the authorship of these oracles, some of which are assigned to an unknown monk named Leontius, who is confused with the "wise" Emperor Leo and the brilliant iconoclast philosopher and mathematician Leo. Scholars have attempted recently to unravel the perplexing agglomeration of these Leonine oracles and bring some order out of the chaotic manuscript tradition.[11] But much yet remains to be done. Paisius deals at considerable length with both the monk Leontius[12] and Leo the Wise whom he confuses with Leo the Mathematician when describing the emperor as "the most wise Leo, Emperor of the Romans, second to Solomon among Christian monarchs, the brilliant mathematician, the geometer, and orator and astrologer who made the famous marble tortoise." [13]

The closer the empire came to its fall in 1453, the more the oracles concerning the inevitable catastrophe circulated, but at the same time the more the prophecies predicting its eventual restoration. Those oracles relating to the last of the Paleologi persisted very strongly until as late as the present century when Greek troops reached the outskirts of Constantinople and advanced into the hinterland of Anatolia in 1920.

After the capture of Constantinople, the oracles and prophecies were diffused widely and read eagerly by the enslaved Greeks. They were altered or adjusted to fit in with contemporary conditions so as to serve as a tonic for national stimulation and rejuvenation. The interpretations were revised with each new development and brought up to date. We find, for instance, that the oracles referring to the duration of the reigns of Byzantine emperors were reinterpreted to apply to the reigns of the Turkish sultans. Many hopes were kindled toward the end of the sixteenth century, when the year 1592 marked the beginning of the eleventh Moslem century.[14] Moreover, with the establishment of the first patriarchate of Moscow three years earlier, the hopes of the Greeks were focused on Russia for eventual salvation. The prophecies concerning the "Fair Race of the North" which would liberate the Christians of the Ottoman Empire seemed to coincide with the rise of Moscovite power. And the Russians soon cultivated the idea for their own political ends. Paisius was among the first of the enlightened Greeks to call upon the czar to free his enslaved countrymen and cited the oracles as proof that they were destined to push back the Turk into the depths of Asia.

An entire line of czars, including the ambitious Peter the Great, fostered the concept in both action and word that the liberation of the Greeks and the subject Christian races of the East would come from Orthodox Russia. Indeed, Russophile Greek oracles continued to cultivate the belief even after the death of Peter, especially during the reigns of Anna (1730–1740) and Elizabeth (1741–1762), and particularly in the early reign of Catharine who had laid the plans for the abortive Greek revolt of 1770. It was during

Czarina Elizabeth's reign that the collection of prophetic sayings under the name of "Agathangelos" made a profound impact on the feelings and imaginations of the common folk.[15]

The failure of the Russians both before and after the Russo-Turkish wars of Catharine II caused a certain wave of disbelief and disillusionment in the reliability of the oracles, especially among those intellectuals who had formerly looked upon the "Fair Race of the North" for salvation. We have seen how Paisius Ligarides attacked the doubting Matthew of Myra for his lack of faith in the oracular utterances, especially those involving Russia.[16] Another such doubter was the encyclopedic Constantine Dapontes (d. 1784), who had placed great faith in those particular Russia-oriented oracles and visions. But after the Muscovite failures he discarded this belief and turned to the Apocalypse of John the Theologian, who had predicted that the empire of the Romans (that is to say, the Greeks) was never destined, in accordance with his interpretation, to be restored, nor were the Russians ever to reign in Constantinople.

Nevertheless, the majority of the Greeks still persisted in their beliefs in prophecies, and in that particular collection of "Agathangelos" which continued to enjoy such widespread popularity even into the twentieth century. So strong was the faith in the infallibility of the ancient and hoary oracles among the Greeks that this was no small contributing factor in the successful outcome of their War of Independence. Following the establishment of their small kingdom, they continued to publish books of prophecies, including the Leonine oracles, and these circulated widely. Besides the many editions of *Agathangelos* there appeared in 1838 in Athens a curious collection edited by Petros Stephanitzes, a friend of Byron, which was given to him in manuscript form by the abbot of a monastery in continental Greece. The death knell of the prophecies and oracles was sounded only in 1922 with the defeat of the Greek armies in Asia Minor, thus bringing to an end forever the dream of the restoration of Constantinople and the Greek Empire and the thousand-year belief in these oracles.

II *Legends*

The most venerated and beloved legend circulating among the Greeks was that concerning the king who had been turned into marble.[16] This story referred to the last of the Greek emperors,

Constantine Paleologus, who fell heroically fighting against the Turks, and it constitutes the core of the Great Idea by which the Greeks were one day destined to recapture Constantinople and resuscitate the lost empire. The advent of the righteous king who had been asleep was of course a popular and widespread folk motif in medieval European messianic literature. The legend, together with many other relevant folk songs and traditions that were born soon after the fall of Constantinople and the dissolution of the empire, were incorporated in the body of oracular and prophetic literature, but with a striking difference. The "enmarbled" or "petrified" king was for the most part not the creation of the cultured Greeks, as in the case of the enigmatic and learned oracles and visions, but of the popular muse, and as such it had more poetic beauty and merit. Those versions of the originally simple legend composed by the learned authors were obviously influenced by ecclesiastical readings, rhetorical turns of phrase, and oracular obscurantism in the traditional manner. But the people's poet had created a beautiful image of a king turned into marble who would one day awaken and avenge the sufferings of his people. Legends of "petrified" women, men, and animals are still common among the Greeks.

The legend of the "petrified" king grew out of the conflicting stories surrounding Constantine Paleologus's death and the disappearance of his body. Paisius incorporated an unknown poet's beautiful rendition in fifteen syllable verse of the death of the beloved emperor:

> The filthy dogs, the Janissaries, slew our beloved king,
> His blood flowed deep and mingled with the blood of many others . . .[17]

Like all Greeks, Paisius was well acquainted with the widespread legend. In one passage he noted that some identified the "hidden king" with the legendary Prester John, a totally different cyclic legend from that of the "petrified king" which had circulated widely in western Europe.[18] Indeed, the belief in the return of some dead hero as a savior existed in most European countries. We need cite but a few. The Albanians, for example, believed that their national hero Skanderbeg would return in time of need, the Serbs that King Markos would do so. There is a striking similarity between the "petrified king" of the Greeks and the German Sigfried or Barbarossa who would return to life. The Swiss, of course, believed that the mythical William Tell, to whom they owed their freedom, along with other patriots, were sleeping an eternal sleep and would awaken whenever Switzerland was threatened. In certain villages in Greece, people persisted in believing, until very recently, that Emperor Constantine would be resurrected for the sake of his country.

Since the legend of the "petrified king" was such a widespread and basic motif which served as a kernel of the regenerative force of the Greeks, eventually developing into the Great Idea, a translation of the folk story would not perhaps be out of place:

> When the time had come for Constantinople to be conquered, and the Turks broke into the city, our king mounted his steed and rushed forth to stop them. The Turks were countless in number, and thousands surrounded him as he struck them down one after the other. But his steed was killed and he fell to the ground. And at the moment that an Arab raised his sword to strike the fallen king, an angel of the Lord appeared and carried him off to a cave deep down in the earth near the Golden Gate.
>
> There the king remains in marble and awaits the moment when the angel will return to waken him. The Turks know this but they cannot find the cave wherein the king awaits. And that is why they built the door through which they know the king will return to recover the city. But when the time will come that the Lord has ordained, the angel will descend into the cave and resurrect the king from the marble, and will place in his hand that same sword which he had once carried into battle. The king will arise and enter the city through the Golden Gate and with his troops will push back the Turk into the depths of the distant East from which he has come. And there will be much massacre in which the calf will swim in blood.[19]

Yet another legend that survived well into the seventeenth century among the Greeks and Slavs concerned Leo the Wise and the wondrous monuments and inventions he had devised. These included the golden plane tree, roaring lions, singing birds, the marble tortoises, and the "Hand of Justice"; the latter was still current in Greece at the end of the nineteenth century. Among others, the chronicle of Dorotheus of Monemvasia, which was first published in 1631 when Paisius was still in Rome, describes the porphyry "Hand of Justice."

Paisius also cites the "Hand of Justice" when describing the marvels of Leo the Wise:

He had built a marble tortoise, and some say two tortoises, that would roam the city and sweep the streets of garbage by swallowing this and hastening to the sea to vomit it out. Then it would return to collect more filth and leave no refuse in the streets of Constantinople. . . . And what can I say about the famous "Hand of Justice" that decided the price of a purchase by clenching its fist. When the hand opened it was a sign that the price was not fair and more coins had to be deposited. . . . And really there were many marvels in the city which were haunted by the all-wise emperor, such as the marble tortoise which swept the streets of the city and the porphyry "Hand of Justice" that passed judgment in any dispute about price. . . .[20]

The popular folk legend concerning the "Hand of Justice" runs as follows:

In Constantinople at the time it was still ours, there was a hand so contrived that it went by the name of the "Hand of Justice," for it was wont to give fair judgment when people could not tell quite which was righteous and just. For instance, all those who could not agree to the price of an item would adjourn to "The Hand." Then the person who was to purchase an article would begin to measure out the coins by dropping them one by one into the palm of the open hand which would close tightly only when it had deemed that a fair price was deposited.

They say that once upon a time someone wanted to buy a mule but the seller had asked too much for it and they could not reach an agreement. So they adjourned to "The Hand" and the client proceeded to drop a coin into the outstretched palm when lo and behold "The Hand" closed tight. All those present were quite astounded by the apparent injustice which they had seen for the first time, since the mule was an excellent beast and worth much more than just one gold piece. But what else could they do, for "The Hand" had so moved, and they of necessity accepted the verdict, and the owner of the mule was forced to surrender it for one gold piece. Now that same evening, when the new owner took the animal to the inn, it suddenly dropped dead. So he flayed it and sold its hide for which he got but one gold piece! Today there survives only the chain from which the "Hand of Justice" was suspended. This chain hangs on an aged tree near a mosque in Constantinople.[21]

The marvelous and the extraordinary never failed to impress the Greeks, especially during the late foreboding Byzantine period immediately before the catastrophe, and throughout the long dark centuries of the Ottoman occupation when countless stories and tales of magic and the miraculous circulated for the most part by word-of-mouth. Yet the learned Greeks, including Paisius, recorded these legends as part of the rich folklore tradition of their race. The Leo legend in particular became a widespread folklore motif throughout the late Middle Ages in both eastern and western Europe. But nowhere more than among the Greeks and Slavs did the wise emperor and the oracles in his name enjoy such an extensive and lasting popularity. From his prophecies stemmed a rich harvest of predictions and stories that kindled the hopes of the subject Greeks and created a popular literary form that endured for more than seven centuries.

CHAPTER 9

The Book of Prophecies

I *The Manuscript Tradition*

THE existence of this singularly curious and valuable manuscript was first noted by scholars in the decade before the turn of the century.[1] It is not an original autograph copy written by Paisius Ligarides, as some have supposed, but one of many copies that were made. The manuscript which is the most complete copy extant rests in the Patriarchal Library of Jerusalem. It is one of the two copies made in 1657 for Macarius, patriarch of Antioch, when that dignitary had met Paisius in the Kosia convent to which the latter had fled in the wake of the unsettled political situation existing in Moldavia in which he had become intricately involved. The copyist was the Greek monk Baba Yani who, like Paisius, was from the island of Chios. It is obvious from the text that he was a good writer and except for certain passages the minuscule script is beautifully written and is remarkably legible. Macarius carried these two copies of the original work to Antioch, one of which eventually found its way to Jerusalem.[2] It appears to have belonged at one time to the learned Ephraim, patriarch of Jerusalem from 1766 to 1771, so this unique copy had been in Jerusalem at least since the time that Ephraim occupied the patriarchal throne of the Holy City.

The bulky volume occupies 296 folios of manuscript, of which, however, 28 are blank leaves. Each leaf measuring 27 by 19 centimeters (10.6 by 7.5 inches) normally contains 29 lines of text enclosed within a red border measuring 0.235 and 0.13 centimeters (9.2 x 5.1 inches).

Paisius divides the work into two basic sections: oracles already fulfilled from Adam to the fall of Constantinople, and those prophecies whose fulfillment was yet to come. The work is prefaced by a dedication to Czar Alexis Michaelovitch, whom he acclaims as the future emancipator of the Greek nation. Translated into Russian, the work appears to have circulated widely, and many copies were scattered throughout the public and private libraries of Russia, at least until the Bolshevik Revolution. There exists also a second copy of the *Book of Prophecies* in Greek,[3] but this is of the early eighteenth century and contains only portions of the original work in ninety-four folios. So in substance the Jerusalem manuscript is the only surviving complete copy in Greek of the work as originally written by Paisius.

Internal evidence indicates that Paisius completed the voluminous work not in 1656, as maintained by most scholars, but in 1654.[4] And it is most probable that he had been collecting his material over a long period of years, even as early as in the thirties, for many of his citations were from sources not available in the East but which existed only in Rome. He mentions, for instance, that Pope Innocent X was still alive.[5] The dedication to Alexis, however, was made in 1656, and this is the only portion of his book composed in that year.

The *Book of Prophecies,* because of its bulk, has never been published. But certain small extracts have appeared in print. The great scholar Papadopoulos-Kerameus, for instance, published the beautiful metrical lament or dirge of Constantinople consisting of one hundred twenty-eight verses in demotic Greek, a literary gem composed by an anonymous poet soon after the great disaster.[6] No more than half a dozen such dirges in verse have survived, and Paisius fortunately has preserved this exceptionally moving and unique lament in poetical form.

A section dealing with the oracles concerning Crete has also been published, but this covers no more than four folios of the manuscript.[7] Legrand published the preface of the Russian translation of 1673,[8] and Mango deals in passing with the Leonine oracles and interpretations given to some of these by the Chiote.[9] Otherwise, the precious copy of the *Book of Prophecies* lies neglected in a corner of the Jerusalem library still awaiting its editor. Fortunately, the manuscript was microfilmed by the Library of Congress and has thus become more readily accessible to future scholars who may want to study the most learned and encyclopedic production with its extensive and valuable bibliographical references and interpretations of obscure oracles.

II *Structure of the Book of Prophecies*

Paisius Ligarides uses the established form of the popular chronicle to write his masterpiece, which he divides into two major sections or books, as has been mentioned already. The first deals with oracles of the past that had been fulfilled and the second with oracles current in his day that were destined to be fulfilled in the future. And in the manner of the popular chroniclers and historians he begins with the Old Testament, then proceeds with Roman history, and ends with Byzantium and the later period in proper chronological order. The central theme, however, is the oracle. We note that in both books he develops in the introductory proems his theories on the significance of prophecies in general and the importance which man attaches to such oracles.

The first book opens with a dedicatory epistle to Czar Alexis in which Paisius calls upon the Russian monarch to liberate the enslaved Greeks since the prophecies had so ordained it. This is followed by an introductory address to the reader in which he explains what had prompted him to write the *Book of Prophecies.* He loses no time in attacking those who put little faith in oracles, singling out in particular Matthew of Myra,[10] whose work he had read in manuscript when in the Danubian principalities. Then the Chiote explains why he decided to make his work available to the public. He points out that he went to great trouble and to great expense to assemble and to interpret the rich oracular lore and to weave it into a harmonious unity much in the manner of a "new Homeric rhapsode." He depicts himself as an industrious bee flitting from source to source collecting and digesting the material to produce the final honeyed work:

> I thought that a treasure that lies hidden away from the world is like a man who has wealth but does not use it and consequently can be considered as lost. And I was urged by friends both high and low alike to produce the work.

The introduction to the reader is followed by three proems or preludes and three prolegomena, the first proem containing the traditional invocation to God because: "It is with God that we began and with God that we end." Here his classical training and pride of race are very evident as he cites the pagan poets and in particular his countryman Homer, who had invoked the muse for inspiration in composing his epics. And like Homer, he too begins his great task by invoking divine providence to guide him through the

> great labyrinthine ways of ancient prophecies concerning Constantinople and the difficult and obscure passages of the oracles in order that I may interpret them or at any rate paraphrase them.

The second and third proems deal at length with the definition of God and once again the author seizes the occasion to display his wide learning on the subject in which he is very much at home as he cites authority after authority, both pagan and Christian. With the conclusion of the definition of God Paisius proceeds in the first prolegomenon with the Holy Scriptures and the meaning of oracles. The second prolegomenon deals with the creation of the world and the etymological derivation of the word God. The prelate was, among other things, an able philologist, but here we find him stretching his argument to a rather untenable point:

> God (the Lord) is a four-letter word because the square is the most stable and solid figure in accordance with the architect and mathematician Vitruvius. And consequently, the various peoples and the languages they use spell out a four-letter word for God. The Jews, for example, use the four-letter Ieoa, the Latins Deus, the Egyptians Toid, the Persians Siri, the Tyrrhenians Asar, the Assyrians Adad, the Turks Alla, the Spaniards Rios, the Germans Gott with two t's, and the Greeks Zeus.

Paisius then gets involved in a disputation with Aristotle in which his philosophical training is put to good use. He brings the chapter to an end with a discussion of the world and the heavens.

The third prolegomenon involves exhaustive treatment of the month and the day on which the world was created. Included are comparative tables of the calendar months used by the Jews, Egyptians, Arab and Turks, Athenians, Macedonians, Cappadocians, and Cypriots. The main body of the first book then follows with forty-one oracles to which are appended the final oracle on events past by the patriarch Scholarius concerning the fall of Constantinople. There is, however, a long insertion consisting of sixteen brief chapters on the "satanic heresies of the Armenians" which intrudes immediately after the thirty-fourth oracle dealing with Emperor Heraclius.[11]

Four literary masterpieces of their kind are appended to conclude the first book, and these include a lament in verse on Constantinople by an unknown poet, a monody in prose by Gennadius Scholarius on the fall of the "New Rome," an elegy in prose by the learned Matthew Camariotes[12] on the same theme, and finally a curious dramatic tale of the young and beautiful maiden Irene with whom Mohammed the Conqueror had fallen in love and for whom he had temporarily abandoned the cares of state. Paisius rounds out the first book by addressing the reader with an epilogue:

> And so, dear reader, you have in a brief manner the outcome of the prophecy which foretold that Mohammed would rule over many nations and devastate the islands and reach as far as the Black Sea. If I did this in a rather cursory manner and not in greater detail, and did not explain everything in a narrative fashion, do not be too critical, for my aim is only to interpret the meanings of the prophecy and not to dwell upon the history of each part. . . . It is not proper that the wise and learned man repeat himself. The historical portions I have added only in passing and this for a better understanding of the oracle. . . . For the proper flow of the book I should perhaps have first recorded the events of the present since this is the natural order . . . but the predictions of the future to me are more important than those of the present, since every person, by his very nature, is more anxious to know the future. Man, being what he is, hungers always to learn something new and to discover things which he had not heard or seen before. Something new always pleases us, much in the way the curious Athenians who were wont to ask when first meeting each other "What's new in the city? . . ."

Paisius then invokes God in eight-syllable verse and makes a further invocation to the Mother of God, the patron saint and protectress of Constantinople, in the same meter, thus bringing the first part of the *Book of Prophecies* to a close.[13]

The second book deals with the oracles concerning future events and the eventual fate of Constantinople. Here again the author introduces the book with three proems one of which unfortunately is missing. It is most probable that the copyist of the manuscript, Baba Yani, had overlooked the second proem either deliberately or under the influence of the daily ration of wine allotted him in lieu of payment for his services. As in the first book, there follow three prolegomena, then a "Brontologium" or "Thunder Book" and the thirteen oracles with two additional prophecies inserted between the eleventh and twelfth oracles. Paisius again explains the attraction of oracles concerning future events:

In his dialogue, Lucian, that curious animal and atheist, chides Hesiod among many others whom he ridiculed. He attacks Hesiod on the grounds that although he had promised to write at length on future events in his "Works and Days," he did not in fact write a single thing about them, but rather, dwelt interminably long with events that had already come to pass. Well, lest I myself be accused of the same thing and appear like an Astydamus or Archilochus dwelling on past events, or like a Pythagorean Harpocrates and a laconic Spartan remaining silent on the most significant events of the future, I have hastened to insert at this point in the book the particular collection of events to come, out of the natural order of things, and then to follow this by the events present in view of the fact that the knowledge of the future is more delightful and desirable to all ages than information on current events which in any case are quite obvious to all. Nor is there much curiosity in examining present events, nor are they read in any earnest for they are quite obvious and have come to pass. After all, people are cognizant of affairs going on around them. When people await the diagnosis by the physician of his patient or the sailor awaits the forecast of the storm, the astrologer the next eclipse of the sun, and, to put it simply, every mathematical computation or physical portent is successfully foretold, and the portent comes to pass, then it is a divine sign to both the learned and the common folk. And the person who made this prediction is called a prophet. . . . Everyone rushes to hear a new teacher with the hope of learning something new and previously unheard. Most people read a new book that has just come out in the belief that they will discover something different and extraordinary. And there is nothing worse for the wise man and scientist than to be famous and talk or write only about old and ancient stories and ignore the new teaching entirely. For it is in the nature of people to love and to wish for new things and to behold and to hear of these.

Why, I ask, do we love the early spring so, the sweet season of spring? Certainly because in all the meadows new flowers appear fresh and verdant on the face of the earth crowning it like stars and beautifying it like pearls.[14]

III *Content of the Book of Prophecies*

Although the central theme of the bulky volume is the oracular tradition, the author uses history as the framework within which to develop his theme. In actual fact, if all the historical passages were removed from the text, these alone would make a voluminous book. It is in the historical passages that we discern the character of the author and his attitude to Mariolatry, to icon worship, to the schism of the churches, to superstition, and so on. And to much in the chronicle tradition he adds tidbits of gossip, rumor, and legend, to make the narrative more attractive to the reader. In the curious passage describing the extent of the domains of the legendary Prester John, for instance, he makes reference to "the isthmus of America" as the westernmost limit of this kingdom." [15] The first small clusters of colonial settlements had been established in America when Paisius wrote this passage.

Icon veneration was practiced as passionately and as commonly by the Greeks of the seventeenth century as in the many centuries before and after. The feelings of Paisius were roused to a high pitch of hatred for the iconoclast emperors of Byzantium who had dared to deny the sanctity of images and the value of icons for the worshiper. He described the significance of icons in the thirty-sixth oracle wherein he stoutly defended iconoduly and displayed an abomination for iconoclasm:[16]

Saint Germanus was the son of a certain archon named Justinian during the reign of Heraclius. Now Constantine Pogonatus, grandson of Heraclius, envied this Justinian and had him murdered. Germanus, his son, was yet a child and he had him castrated lest he some day become a claimant to the throne, and turned him over to the school to be taught the divine and sacred letters. So brilliant was this young lad that eventually he wrote many works which he dedicated to the church of Christ. For his virtue and learning he was appointed patriarch. This Germanus defended icon veneration by arguing that images were not idols and were not contaminated by being kissed, but rather that the worshippers became sanctified and were enlightened by them much in the manner in which one gets warmed by nearing the fire.

But this Emperor Leo did not wish to hear of it. On the contrary, he only confirmed what the prophetic holy fathers had predicted, that he would be an iconoclast. And so after slapping the holy patriarch across the face, he passed an edict that the sacred images were no longer to be worshipped. Now the Christian emperors had in the city a royal university with twelve students in zealous imitation of Christ and the Apostles. The professor taught in a building belonging to the palace near Saint Sophia and at this school there existed at that time a collection of 700,000 books. When the mad and impious emperor observed that he could not convert either the patriarch or the professor to his way of thinking, he ordered the university to be burned to the ground together with the professor, his students and all the library of books. Then he removed the most holy Germanus from the patriarchal throne and in his place installed one Anastasius, who believed as he did, and who started the iconoclastic struggle by inciting both the emperor and the people against image worship.

In the 24th year of his reign on the day of the feast of Saint Demetrius, there took place a terrible earthquake in the city that felled many columns of the emperor including the column of the Emperor Arcadius which was situated at the Xerolofos. The Emperor Leo fell ill with such a bad case of dysentery that all his inners were dissolved and he gave up his foul ghost to join those other demons Judas and Julian the Apostate. His son Constantine Copronymus who became emperor after him had befouled the holy baptismal font by relieving himself during the baptismal ceremony at which the Patriarch Germanus officiated. From this incident Germanus foretold and correctly predicted that much evil would befall the Christians and the church of Christ at this man's hands, as indeed subsequently happened. For this man blasphemed the Mother of God Mary by maintaining that after she gave birth to Christ she was no longer holy and did not deserve much honor, just as when a chest is emptied of its precious stones it no longer has any value.

But no, no, you impious one! The bottle that is full of perfume still smells beautifully when it is emptied. And a trunk that is packed with musk does not cease to retain the scent of musk when it is emptied of its contents.

This great sinner ordered that all the saints should not be called saints but be referred to as the martyr George, for instance, or the pious Antony, and no respect or honor should be given them, nor to the Mother of God, and that whenever sacred relics were found they be trodden upon and dishonored.

So let those who today do not accept the intervention of the saints be ashamed of themselves.

Like most Greeks, Paisius believed that God was the active agent in history and that each kind of behavior had its inevitable consequence of reward or punishment. The notion of retribution was strongly embedded in the Greek conscience, and Paisius cites several examples from history to support the doctrine of divine retribution, which was yet another pagan survival among the many that had been incorporated into the Greek Orthodox church:

This Empress Irene had brought peace finally to the body of the church. The honor, respect and veneration that icons had formerly enjoyed were reintroduced by her. And the attacks by the iconoclasts came to an end. But she made one big mistake. Deceived like a new Eve by the malicious seeds of intrigue and the thirst for power, she wanted to reign as sole ruler and devised means by which to have her own son blinded. Her son was a worthy young man and very brave in battle. Now when he was deprived of his sight, the sun darkened for seventeen days and refused to emit any rays of light to those who had so unjustly deprived the young emperor of his light. So dark had it become that ships which were sailing in the area lost their bearings in the fog and darkness.

I never cease to marvel at the supreme justice of God and the manner of retribution for those who have suffered. Exactly five years later to the day and the month when he had blinded his uncles and Alexius, the emperor himself was blinded by his mother Irene, and recompense was thus pitilessly made. But Irene eventually was deprived of her empire. She was sent to live in exile in Mitylene where she spent her time spinning wool until she died. In such manner does the good judge exact retribution from the unjust.[17]

Yet Paisius was not all that naive to attribute an historical episode to divine power or influence alone. As an accomplished historian, he sought for more realistic causes for the fall of Constantinople and the ensuing enslavement of his race. He wracked his brains, as he says, to find what sins and lawlessness his forefathers had committed to bring on the long slavery of the Greeks and the heavy burden of Turkish tyranny which had now endured two hundred and three years, and was going from bad to worse. And he concludes that there were ten basic causes which had brought about the eclipse of the Greek Empire.

The first was injustice. Bribery and harsh taxes compounded with changes in the old established customs and mores weakened the state. Aristocrats were degraded and humiliated; the vulgar were promoted to high positions. Innovations, he maintained, were always harmful and dangerous. The inhabitants of Asia Minor welcomed the Turks and many of the Christian inhabitants converted to Islam because they found that the crude and inhuman barbarians were far more sympathetic to their suffering and were more humane than their own countrymen.

Another cause for the loss of empire was the love of luxury and the pursuit of pleasure. Lack of political stability and harmony, and petty jealousies were further reasons for the dissolution. Evil in the leaders, civil wars, ambition, invitation to the Turks for intervention in Byzantine affairs, miserliness in supporting and maintaining an army and navy, mistrust, cruelty, the devaluation of the coinage, and finally the lack of learning and virtue, were all factors contributing to the downfall.

From his description of what in his mind brought on the miserable condition of the Greeks, Paisius emerges as an ultraconservative in politics and a stuffed shirt opposed to innovations in any shape or form. Ironically enough, however, although he had the habit of expounding at great length on the virtues of the good Christian, he himself fell far short of these ideals. He was a very obvious hypocrite who had carried the outer semblances of an Orthodox hierarch but who throughout his stormy career had been guilty of some of those very vices against which he preached.

His own hypocrisy comes to the surface again when he describes the attempts for the union of the Greek and Latin churches.[18] It goes without saying that he had felt deeply about the failure of the union and one can presume that his vitriolic attacks against the Lutherans, and the Protestant church in general, were motivated more by his strong pro-Catholic sentiments than by his Orthodoxy. The Protestant churches had been laying the ground for a possible rapprochement with the Greek church in the seventeenth century and forming some kind of common front to fight the infiltration of the Jesuits. But these attempts had come to nothing.

When the Emperor John died, Manuel Paleologue became ruler. He also visited Italy to solicit help from the westerners, but when he refused to kiss the icon of Christ which was woven into the sleeve of the vestment worn by the bishop conducting the service, he failed to get either help or understanding. With his one-eyed wife Helen, a fine and virtuous woman, he begot six sons, John, Theodore, Constantine, Demetrius, Thomas, and Andronicus the leper. Manuel died at the advanced age of 105 and his first-born son John became Emperor.

John was a prudent and judicious ruler. Seeing that his empire was on the verge of being swallowed up by the Moslem wolf and that Constantinople was the only citadel remaining in his hands, he took the Patriarch Joseph, a saintly and wise man, together with his chatterbox archpriests and chosen Greek advisers to hold a common meeting with the Latins to talk about various matters which had been previously discussed concerning possible union of the churches.

The details of what happened then are recorded in the minutes of the Florentine synod wherein all the signatures of the dignitaries appear except that of Eugenius Marcus, Bishop of Ephesus and patriarchal exarch. Though he was asked by the other fathers of the synod whether he would affix his signature, he replied very skillfully and ambiguously that everyone had signed, so how could it be that he had not? In other words, if everyone had signed, how is it possible that he could not have signed. But later on, he removed his cloak of hypocrisy and the manner of his ambiguous reply by declaring that he had replied negatively and not affirmatively; that is to say, everyone signed but not he, trying to show in this way that he was the only one who did not wish to accept the Latin dogma. After this he went to Crete and wrote against the ruling of the Florentine Council where he declared that the Holy Ghost proceeded from only the Father. As a result, the schism of the churches and the gap that had separated them widened even further.

A much more vivid indication of his pro-Catholic sentiments emerges in the thirty-ninth oracle wherein he describes the schism of the churches:

There is an oracle ascribed to Theophilus, Roman presbyter and cleric of the Great Church of Rome, which oracle translated into the Greek from the Latin by John Zygabinus reads as follows: "A schism will arise in the church of God. Then there shall exist two nuptials, one lawful and the other adulterous. The adulterous marriage will reign and Satan will rejoice. The ecclesiastic will not be named and the lawful nuptials will take flight and not be found."

Now to what schism could Theophilus be referring, the partial and particular one that occurred in the Western Church when there existed a lawful Pope and an adulterous anti-Pope? Or that well-known schism which took place between the Western and Eastern churches? An overwhelming doubt seizes me and I am more passionately anxious to hear what others say rather than present my own thoughts in writing.

But one thing I do know for a fact. The ruinous and miserable schism of the churches occurred in the year of Our Lord 878, that is, when Photius reassumed the patriarchal throne as a result of which a synod was summoned and he was anathematized as an adulterer because he had removed the most holy Patriarch Ignatius from the throne and had occupied it himself like a thief in the night, not obtaining it through the normal channels, and he forgave Caesar Bardas who was justly anathematized by Ignatius since he had abandoned his lawfully wedded wife and lived publicly in sin with his mistress, thus committing open adultery in violation of his nuptial vows.[19]

Paisius carried on in the same vein with the history of the first schism and the temporary lull in the polemics between the churches following the death of Ignatius. But we discover that the adamant Photius poured more fuel into the fire. Paisius adds other causes for the break between the churches, such as the rivalry between Rome and Constantinople for control of Bulgaria, the hostile attitude of the fiery Patriarch Cerularius and the crowning of Charlemagne by the pope. The gist of the presentation by Paisius is that the schism should never have taken place. Until the time he had written his *Book of Prophecies,* Paisius found it difficult to shed his Catholic bias. Curiously enough, however, some ten years later when in Russia, the Chiote had a complete change of heart because he saw in Photius the great inspirer and the foremost ecclesiastic of the Greek Orthodox church.

In many respects Paisius was admirably fitted to be the historian of his times. His varied travels had given him a considerable firsthand knowledge of the peoples and localities with which his narrative is concerned. His Greek background and his close association with both the Catholics and the Orthodox enabled him to understand and to appreciate both sides of the important religious and moral questions of his day. And lastly, his intimate knowledge of the vast sources from which he could draw, both published and in manuscript, accorded him exceptional opportunities to acquire accurate information.

On the other hand, his personal preferences and prejudices were strong. An opportunist by nature, he lacked the studious scholarship and objectivity which are so necessary to the ideal historian. All these qualifications and demerits of its author are exhibited in the *Book of Prophecies.* It has unquestioned merits but at the same time unquestioned defects. It should not be forgotten, however, that these defects are more than balanced by positive excellencies in the work.

Paisius was so much more than a historian, a collector and interpreter of oracles, a theologian, antiquarian, mathematician, astronomer, geographer, and etymologist that we can regard him as an encyclopedist with an unquenchable thirst for knowledge. He was hardly modest, however, and was forever fond of displaying his learning on all points. We discover that he had a remarkable memory and could quote extensive passages from authors whom he had read many years before and whose works were not readily accessible at the time he wrote his *Book of Prophecies.* There are inconsistencies and a few omissions in his masterpiece, and he fails to mention certain facts of material importance. But such imperfections are due not so much to the lack of information as to lack of care and much reliance on memory work. It was wholly natural that he should write it section by section, as time went on, instead of writing it at one sitting. A certain looseness of the connection between all the parts can be justified by the very nature of the work and the manner in which he moulded it into a unity. His defective workmanship can be accounted for to some degree by his change of attitude to the Greek Orthodox church, especially when he became deeply involved in the affairs of that church in the Balkans and Russia. His wavering between the Catholic and the Orthodox faiths, and his divided loyalties, may excuse the failure to weld together more smoothly the successive portions of his history.

Yet, when all is said and done, it is by reading his *Book of Prophecies* that we can know him, not so much as a Catholic or an Orthodox theologian, but as an enlightened Greek of the Ottoman period, with all the attributes and shortcomings of a race that had lost an empire but had not lost its identity or its faith in eventual liberation from oppressive enslavement. When Paisius dedicated his work to Czar Alexis of Russia, the Greeks had been living under the domination of the Turks for over six generations and they were destined to endure yet another six generations of the hated occupation before they could breathe freely once again. The *Book of Prophecies* and similar works did much to keep alive this faith in eventual salvation.

III *City of Cities*

Constantinople, the city of cities, the center of the universe to the Greeks, the crossroads of the world that had as many churches as the year had days, was the natural capital of the Greek Orthodox world since it was first established by Constantine the Great. Athens had long before sunk into oblivion, forgotten, or, at best, remembered only vaguely by a handful of learned scholars acquainted with the classical heritage. The city on the Bosphorus had become the center of all Greek aspirations, the navel of the Byzantine and post-Byzantine world. Its fall made a lasting and deep impression on the Greek and had dominated his every thought and feeling. It gave rise to a large corpus of laments, dirges, and wailing songs, which make up one of the main themes of literary creativity during the Ottoman period. Paisius describes the world-shaking event in his own words modeled on the style of the historians and chroniclers who had recorded the tragic event before him.

> The Turks entered Constantinople as victors. But dear heart, do not break asunder when you hear of the suffering and the mourning that this caused. They left nothing undone. They slew both young and old. They did not spare the children. They took no pity on the pregnant. They did not respect the aged. They dishonored virtuous women. They deflowered the virgins. They raped the young men. They beat the monks. They dragged the priests through the streets. They defiled the churches. They scattered the relics. They smashed the icons. They turned the sacristies into stables for their horses. Tremble O earth! Shudder O sun! Weep ye stars! Cloud over and darken ye skies! Whose heart can be so stony as to control the flow of tears and not weep for such pillage and destruction of once the most blessed and happiest of cities. . . . Whose heart is so wrought of iron as not to ache at such disaster?

One sees through the eyes of Paisius the passionate attachment and nostalgia of the Greeks for the great metropolis on the Bosphorus. He never tired of hearing or reading of its marvels, its monuments, its wealth and beauty. The architectural jewel of the city, the foremost temple of the Eastern Orthodox world, Saint Sophia, or the Church of the Holy Wisdom, became the symbol around which the unredeemed Greeks created legends and stories that permeated their every thought. The great city and Saint Sophia were the dominant themes in what little literary creation came out of the four dark unproductive centuries of Turkish rule. Both the folk poet and the learned theologian dreamed that the mass which had been so abruptly interrupted on May 29, 1453, in Saint Sophia would some day be resumed:

> It is related that when Constantinople was taken, the sun was darkened not because of an eclipse but as a sign from God that the brilliant throne of the East had set. . . . The Jewish traveler Benjamin who lived at the time of Manuel Paleologus records that the city was, next to Baghdad, the largest in the world. It had as many churches as the year has days. Exceptionally outstanding was the grand Church of the Holy Wisdom, the heaven on earth, the throne of the glory of God according to Choniates, which had columns of silver and of gold, the pulpit alone for which was spent the sum of 3,650 centinaria of gold equal to the entire annual income of Egypt. It had 90 priests to conduct the liturgy and 150 members in its choir. Woe to me, it has become a temple of the Turks! The first Moslem to pollute it was the Sultan Mohammed who ordered, alas, according to Isidore, Metropolitan of Russia, that the central image of Christ be destroyed together with the True Cross and the other holy images and icons. The holy and divine Bible was exorcized and the other books were strewn about, and the priestly robes were profaned. The holy utensils were polluted by the Turks according to Leonardus who adds that the Turks also carried the crucified Christ out into the streets and paraded Him through the city spitting and cursing and mocking Him with laughter, saying, "Here is the God of the Christians." But blessed be Your forbearance O Christ the King and gentle Lord.[20]

Since the *Book of Prophecies* has as its theme the oracles past, present, and future, concerning Constantinople, the author naturally devotes much space to the history of the city, the date of its foundation, and its eventual fate. Paisius knew both the old Rome and the "New Rome" and it is interesting to see which of the two in his mind was the more beautiful. Rather, however, than commit himself to the one or to the other, he very adroitly evades the issue by quoting the views of numerous others and dwells at length on the founding of the city. At the same time, he gives us some idea of the vast bibliographical sources that he had at hand:

> Eutychianus the Grammarian, Eutropius the Sophist, Eleusius the Philosopher, Troilus, and Hesychius Tachygraphus all assert that Constantine, son of Constans, founded the New Rome in the three-hundredth sixty-second year from the reign of the Caesar Augustus.

Some maintain that Byzas the king had built the walls of Byzantium with the help of Poseidon and of Apollo, but these are fantasies because it was in fact through the inspiration of God. And Constantine Manasses relates in his political verse that it was at God's wish. He had abandoned the idea of Chalcedon, Thessaloniki, and Troy itself, each of which he had planned to build as his new capital, and according to Glycas and Zosimus, when the eagles had picked up the stones and other building materials and flew them from Troy to the shore opposite at the beautiful site of Byzantium, he decided on the latter place. So let Chios pride herself in the fact that it was named after the snow which fell from the sky when it was first being built, and Rhodes in the beautiful rose which appeared when it was first settled, and Athens in the olive, Lacedemon in the horse, the Roman capitoleum in the skull, and other cities and countries in their various monstrous signs, for Byzantium does not boast of any tree or bird, but only in divinely sent and indubitable portents that had appeared when it was first being built.

As Nicephorus Callistus relates in the eighth book of his ecclesiastical history, when the most Christian Constantine wished to build the city and encircle it with walls, he saw an angel of the Lord walking before him. When one of his attendants asked how far he would walk, he replied as far as his guide and mentor wished it, for according to the chronographer, when the Emperor wished to mark out the city limits he was at great loss as to whether it should be small or large. And in a dream he had, he saw an angel of the Lord who spoke to him and said that he should not worry about building the new city. So when the Emperor awoke next morning he summoned his chief builder and asked that he accompany him and that wherever he walked he should mark out the boundaries of the city. At the moment that he bade his builder to do this, and just as the angel had told the Emperor in the dream that he would guide him in the morning and that the Emperor should follow him and delineate the limits of the site, he laid out the walls of the city as far as he went. So in this manner the angel proceeded ahead and no one could see him but the monarch. Then behind the Emperor followed the chief builder who marked out the boundary of the walls which is the limit of the city even today.

Euphratas whom the Emperor provided with much money supervised the construction of the city which he built with much zeal and pride, erecting many and large residences with fine courtyards as remarkable and as beautiful as the aristocrats had in Rome, so much so in fact that when they came to settle there from the old Rome they were amazed and had to admit that the edifices were practically identical, in accordance with what Codinus writes, and indistinguishable from their own palaces. The ladies of the leading families of Rome were brought to the New Rome by a ruse and after their ships arrived at the new city wherein they were to take up their residence they exclaimed that they had returned to their former home city of Rome, so identical were the residences and palaces.

Just as Tacitus maintains that the old Rome was divided into fourteen districts, so does Gilius say that the New Rome contained fourteen quarters. Constantinople also has 24 gates, just as many courts as the Athenians had, the number corresponding to the 24 elements. Laonicus Chalcocondyles writes that the city is shaped like a triangle and resembles the very royal eagle when it spreads its wings in flight. . . . Indeed, the great Augustine spoke very rightly when he said that the Supreme God deigned that another, a new Rome, be built to be the daughter or the companion of the Roman Empire. Hence the double-headed eagle became the symbol for the one and the other Rome united in one empire. That is why I do not agree with Codinus when he says that the rule of the old Rome ceased when the New Rome was built, for they are not different but one and the same, just as a mother and daughter do not differ but have the same relationship one to the other. And if Sozomen thinks the New Rome more beautiful than the old, on the contrary Suidas argues that the old Rome is more beautiful than the new. But they do vie with each other in both beauty and in honor.

And in fact what did the old Rome have that the new did not have? Both had capitolea, a hippodrome, theater, hunting lodge, portico, forum . . . Great portents and omens occurred in both old and New Rome and both Romes suffered good and bad luck and even to this day in these cities people fall easily into prosperity or into misery.[21]

IV *Rhetorical Devices and Etymology*

A favorite figure of speech occurring frequently in the *Book of Prophecies* and in most of his major works is the simile. Paisius makes great use of this rhetorical figure and here again we see the strong influences of both his classical and theological heritages at work. Of the ancients, he has constant recourse to Homer, his compatriot (in his eyes, at least), whom he frequently quotes and never ceases to consciously imitate. From the master poet Paisius derives his fondness for the simile, onomatopoeia, parechesis, ornamental epithets, and other tricks of the epic poet's art. In the age of Paisius, Homeric studies had moved rapidly ahead in western Europe, and together with the Old Testament, Homer's and Virgil's works more than any other, had become the training manuals for most European intellectuals. In the twenty-third oracle concerning the horoscope of Constantinople, for example, wherein Paisius plunges into astrology and the signs of the zodiac, he writes:

> The whole world is the house of God. And the mountains around the world are its walls, the heavens its domes, the stars its skylights, the constellations its paintings and all the meadows its grounds.[22]

In yet another passage in which he attempts an interpretation of an oracle attributed to Leontius concerning the imperial family of the Lascarids, he says:

> Just as the rose stands upright and fresh during the day and withers away next morning, so did the family of the Lascarids like a fair and pure rose blossom forth only to disintegrate like the rose.[23]

Further on, he uses a poetic turn of phrase to describe springtime as "when the hands of spring paint the earth with flowers." [24]

On etymology, one of his favorite sciences, Paisius shows occasional penetration, but many of his derivations approach the absurd. The town of Trikkala was so called because it had three outstanding features, that is, springs, fruitful vines, and high hills.[25] The Emperor Constantine Pogonatus was given the epithet because he was clean shaven when he left for Sicily, but when he returned to Constantinople he was sporting a beard.[26] Saracens derive their name from a geographical region in Arabia called Sara, according to one authority.[27] The Agars (Turks) and the Saracens are one and the same race from Arabia. One of the more absurd derivations is that of the Morea, the medieval and modern name for the Peloponnese:

> They [the Moors of Spain] raided all the Dodecanese, not sparing even the well-known island of Chios, and the famous Peloponnese which is called the Morea after the Moors who conquered it, by which name it is still called today.[28]

Etymologists today account for the name either by the shape of the peninsula which resembles the mulberry leaf (the *morea* in Greek) or by the abundance of the mulberry trees in that region.

Over and above its purely historical and literary merits, the *Book of Prophecies* is especially important in that it provides further evidence of the firm belief and confidence existing among the oppressed Greeks that eventually they would be freed with the help of God and the intervention of the Christian powers of Europe. These hopes and desires, born directly after the fall of Constantinople and the dissolution of the Greek Empire, emerge in verse, in song, and in legendary traditions. Later, when the faith in eventual fulfillment of these hopes was firmly established, it appeared in the form of new oracles and prophetic visions. It is indeed remarkable that this optimism was born so soon after the fall, when all had been lost and no glimmer of hope in future salvation existed. But the great calamity of the Greeks occurred precisely at that juncture where fear and desperation gave way to hope and nascent courage. Before the catastrophe, the prophecies of the future were ill-omened and spoke of terrible doom and suffering, but immediately after the event these were full of expectation. The pendulum of history had made a full upward swing from the depressed and desperate state in which the Greeks found themselves to a high point of optimism and faith in their future, attaining a climax in the "Visions of Agathangelos" in the eighteenth century, which had made such a tremendous impact upon the morale and the spirit of the enslaved Greeks. The *Book of Prophecies* belongs to what we can call the Middle Period of the oracular tradition, falling between the extreme depression accompanying the fall of Constantinople to the high point of optimism attained by the "Visions of Agathangelos."

Paisius devotes much space to the "Oracles of Leo the Wise," particularly those in the spoken or demotic Greek, which had enjoyed such wide popularity among the subject Christians of the Ottoman Empire in the sixteenth century and later. But he attributes these to the monk Leontius. Some of the oracles deal with the dissolution of the Byzantine Empire, whereas others concern the ultimate liberation of the city on the Bosphorus.[29] The author quotes the appropriate passage, then cites the interpretation given by an anonymous scholiast, and adds either his own explanation or that of another scholiast.

The same group of prophecies hints at the reconquest of Constantinople from the Latins by Michael Paleologus, his efforts to unite the churches, the Florentine Council, the defeat of Sultan

Bayazid at the hands of Tamerlane the Great, and the fall of Constantinople.[30] The eventual liberation is described in the same cycle of Leonine oracles. Constantinople, he says, will be liberated by an alliance of the Christian nations. He disagrees with one interpretation given by the scholiast to the twelfth oracle concerning future events, and substitutes the Austrians (who were to prove the most anti-Greek and Turkophile power in Europe) for the Persians. The symbolic lion of the oracle is the king of Spain, the leopard is the king of Poland, the basilisk is the czar of Muscovy, the fox is Venice, and the wolf represents the king of France. In the same oracle, the falcon is the "Fair Race," according to Gennadius Scholarius and this, of course, refers to the Russians. Paisius adds a further oracle attributed to Saint Daniel the Stylite on the eventual liberation of Constantinople through the combined efforts of the Christian powers.

Paisius Ligarides is not content merely to be a collector of oracles and of miscellaneous and curious facts. It is true, he has a great number of these at his command; they come readily enough to point a moral or to warn against evil. But he makes them pass through the crucible of his mind so as to form a unity of his own creation and not a collection that he has merely compiled. In the various prolegomena and proems of the *Book of Prophecies,* each of which constitutes a self-contained unity in essay form, he attempts to derive the general laws and the universal truths underlying the events of history and the vicissitudes in natural fortunes. Each of the numerous chapters is a self-contained whole, but each in turn is linked in masterly fashion to the thread of the bulky work devoted to the oracular tradition, with the underlying theme being the liberation of his race from the abominous yoke of the Moslem oppressor. It can be assumed that to combine primacy in literature with pre-eminence in theology is rarely successful, despite Chateaubriand's argument that "of all religions which ever existed, the Christian religion is the most poetic, the most human, the most favourable to liberty, arts and letters, and that the modern world owes everything to it." [31]

Probably Paisius has combined the two more dexterously on the whole than most of his contemporaries. He chose the chronicle form of history in which his race excelled within which to incorporate the oracles, and he brought it almost to perfection.

CHAPTER 10

Epilogue

MODERN history begins with the fall of Constantinople in the year 1453. The history of modern Greece also begins in the same year. Western Europe was shaken by the disastrous event, yet it was but a thunderstorm before the dawn. The dispersal of Greek scholars to the Italian peninsula and the North opened anew the literature and science of the older world at a time when the creative energy of the Middle Ages seemed to have sunk into exhaustion. The fifteenth century could boast of little liberal art and science. But the two centuries that followed were perhaps the most brilliant in the world's entire history. The seeds of classical Greece, planted by the Byzantine carriers, soon bore a rich harvest. Despite the exhausting and destructive wars of the seventeenth century, art, literature, science, philosophy, faith, and morals, had all throbbed with a rejuvenated life and energy, and Europe stumbled within a few generations into a new and undiscovered world.

But in the East, the Greeks maintained a precarious existence through an interminable period of trials more cruel and terrible than any of their ancestors could have dreamed. Thanks to the church and the people whose hearts had beat as one, an identity was maintained. The inextinguishable and unflagging devotion to the Ecumenical Orthodox church acted from an early period in Byzantine times and for many centuries thereafter as an ark of safety and a means of identity. It is easily understood that the state of things under the Turks was not favorable to the cultivation of a rich literary heritage and to the maintenance of a purity of speech, either among the learned or the unlearned classes. Hence, the literary revival of the seventeenth century, when the language of modern Greece began to assume a more fully developed form, occurred in areas that were not yet occupied by the Ottomans, particularly in Crete and the Ionian Islands, and among the Greeks of the diaspora in Italy, in such centers as Venice, Rome, and Padua. The modern language, it is true, was forming itself from as early as the eleventh century or roughly from A.D. 1000 to 1600, during which period certain modern forms were ousting the corresponding ancient forms. And it is certain that the popular speech of the Byzantine Empire possessed all the grammatical peculiarities which mark the language of Greek as spoken and written at the present day.

I *Modern Language and Literature*

The modern language came into literary use very slowly and with much difficulty. This was due to the extreme conservatism of Greek writing. The Byzantine character, in fact, lay behind the development of the language.[1] Existing Greek texts dating from the twelfth to the seventeenth centuries make evident that the struggle between the spoken and the older written style was very acute. The feeling for the older, conservative type of Greek led writers into faults, and we find much ignorance and use of barbarisms. These texts were written in a language of mixed and contradictory character. The authors of these works, who spoke a language closely akin to the Greek of today, were under the influence of the classical, written tradition, which they found difficult to shed. Their language as a consequence was a mass of inconsistencies in grammatical style and vocabulary. Archaisms and barbarisms occur side by side with everyday speech. The long process of development was not so much the formation of a modern spoken language as a slow demoticizing of the written language as modern spoken Greek gradually forced itself into written use.

For the history of the Greek language, therefore, the texts of the seventeenth century assume a basic importance. In the language that Paisius Ligarides used, we recognize a mixture of the Greek that he heard every day and of the Byzantine classical style that was itself a prolongation of the old *koine* of the New Testament. This style was to most writers awkward and artificial. They had learned it in school, had heard it in the liturgy, had used it by rote and formula in rhetoric, but it was inevitable, unless they were especially good scholars and linguists (and these were few and far between) that they would make many errors. At the moment when Paisius was busy drafting his *Book of Prophecies,* the only literary creations that were free of barbarisms and were in fact pure modern Greek were the remarkable Cretan epics and the ballads of continental Greece. The Cretan love story *Erotocritos*, containing ten thousand verses of melodic fifteen syllables, was composed at the time Ligarides was in the Danubian principalities. The Greeks had never lost the instincts of a poetic race. In four centuries of what we could call the "Greek Dark Ages," extending from the fall of Constantinople to the eve of the War of Independence, poetry was the only literary form that had matured and attained such perfection. Prose, with few exceptions, as in the historical chronicles, continued for long to be a confounding mixture of Byzantine, ecclesiastical, and spoken Greek, subsequently enriched by Venetian and Turkish accretions to the vocabulary. In commenting on how he interpreted the cryptic and apocryphal oracles, Paisius asks the reader not to be shocked by the number of "mixo-barbaric" words because "in the time of Leo the Wise such a mixed language was used. Even Constantine Porphyrogenitus in his book on the Themes used such barbarisms." [2]

The ballads, folk songs, chronicles, and oracles belonging to a period extending from the eleventh to the eighteenth centuries supply the link of connection between the popular literature of the late Byzantine Empire and that of modern Greece. Besides their literary interest, however, they possess considerable historical value, for they are one of the most important sources for the history of the Greek people under Turkish dominion. But for them, the four centuries that cover the Greek Dark Ages would be almost a blank as far as the life of the Greek people is concerned. They throw much light on the obscure centuries about which comparatively few and precious accounts have reached us.

The emergence of the modern language in its written form owes much to the Greeks of Italy. Their tendency was to publish books with a practical utility, so these were of necessity written in the spoken Greek of the day. This tendency to write in a plain language is equally apparent in the theological works. The intellectuals believed that the Greek should be educated in a language understood by him, and the establishment of Greek presses in the seventeenth century in Italy was directly related to the multiplication of publications in popular Greek that circulated at the time. Translations of the ancient authors were made in the spoken language, and the first bilingual dictionaries of the "Romaic," or popular idiom, began to appear. Translations of the European classics also issued off the press in increasing number for the edification of the Greeks, together with grammars, geographies, and arithmetic books. Church rhetoric, in contrast with the other forms of rhetoric, did not cease to thrive in the East. The proselytizing efforts of the papacy reinforced the development of this form of prose. The cultivation of oratory among the eastern theologians was the direct result of the attempts made by the Roman church to return the "renegade and schismatic" Greeks to the fold. We thus find that western propaganda and the cultivation among the Greeks of the desire for freedom appeared to walk arm in arm. But together with these two the awareness of an unbroken continuity of the classical and medieval Greek heritage also grew.

What emerges from the attempts of the Catholic church in general and of the Jesuits in particular to proselytize the Orthodox is the striking fact that the change in church allegiance did not mean a diminishing of loyalty to the race and its heritage. We discover that the Greeks who had embraced Catholicism were very active in the affairs and the problems of their kinsmen. They had changed their dogma, not to deny the race, but rather to be able the better and more effectively to serve it. Without a doubt some opportunists existed among these Greeks—after all, the papacy showered titles and high positions generously on the renegades—but these were in a minority.

The outstanding intellectual of this group was Leo Allatius, the mentor of Paisius Ligarides. Though a fanatical papist, he had never abandoned his Greek conscience and concern for the lot of his countrymen. Most of his many volumes of works were written in the Latin tongue, but when he addressed his compatriots he did so in the popular language which they could understand. Paisius Ligarides followed in the footsteps of his master. Like him, his knowledge ranged far and wide into literature, history, archeology, philosophy, and theology; and like him he was deeply concerned and eventually deeply involved with the fortunes of the Greeks. But unlike Leo Allatius, Paisius finally returned to the fold of the eastern Orthodox church.

II *Conclusion*

Paisius Ligarides of Chios was born one hundred and fifty-seven years after the fall of Constantinople and died one hundred and fifty-seven years before the seat of government of the newly formed Kingdom of Greece was moved to Athens. His life thus spans the middle period of the four centuries of Turkish domin- ion, and his lifetime marks in many ways the turning point in the history of modern Greek literature. The first works began to issue from the pen of intellectuals, while the ballads and romances in poetic verse and folk tales had already attained a maturity and literary perfection in both content and form. The Greeks began sluggishly but inevitably to emerge from the deep mire of de- spondency and depression into which they had fallen to acquire a stronger and more resolute sense of national identity and purpose. This identity took firm root in the dark years of Turkish occupa- tion and slowly gathered momentum to bloom forth in open rebel- lion against the detested tyrant. The Orthodox church was most instrumental in cultivating the national feelings of the Greeks, and Paisius Ligarides was one of a handful of intellectual clergymen who contributed much in helping the church in its efforts to nour- ish the soul and mind of its flock and to inculcate the feeling for freedom.

The renegade prelate returned to his people and to his church after many years of service in the ranks of the papacy. Through- out his works we detect the hesitancy and doubt that had plagued his conscience. Although he had received a thorough training in Catholicism, at heart he was always a Greek, and his feelings for his race eventually carried him back into the arms of the Orthodox church wherein he could best serve his people. When finally he closed his eyes—a lonely, friendless old man in distant Kiev—he did so with the vision of a new Greece, freedom for his country- men, and at the same time with repentance in his soul for the sins he had committed. Paisius had lived to hear rumors of the exist- ence of the first bands of irregular warriors in the still uncon- quered mountain fastnesses of Greece; he had seen the birth of a new national literature; and he had witnessed the victory of the Greek rite in the Orthodox church of Russia.

Driven by an inner urge to write for the edification of his fellow Greeks, Paisius conceived the unique *Book of Prophecies,* the only work of its kind in the entire corpus of modern Greek literature. In range, in composition, content, and substance, as well as in form, this masterpiece is didactic in character; that is to say, it brings to mind an oratorical exercise delivered from the pulpit. It is in many ways also a panegyrical homily on the life and death and eventual resurrection of Constantinople. It can be described almost as a lengthy funeral oration. Abandoning the Latin language in which he was trained and in which he could write with equal ease, Paisius returned to his mother tongue to express his innermost thoughts, and this he did most effectively in a consistent and smoothly flowing grammatical style. He turned unhesitatingly to the language of the common man, although the book was addressed to both learned and unlearned alike. It is true that he borrowed from a vast collection of authors, classical, biblical, and Byzantine; but the extracts from these sources he wove together using the oral tradition and the popular legends as the thread. The work has something of the oral form as well. It could be read aloud to an audience with good effect. The author enjoyed the sound and the substance of the word, for which he had great feeling. From the point of view of language, he is one of the purer demotic writers of the Ottoman period, even though the language of prose, unlike that of poetry, had not yet been formed. The foreign words he uses are very limited in number, in contrast with subsequent Greek literary productions; and when they are used, either Turkish or Venetian, he does so to add color to the narrative.

Every literary work is examined, judged, and defined by its external form. Irrespective of whether the *Book of Prophecies* has a didactic or edifying aim, it possesses an original literary form all its own, created by an imaginative author to give the effect of a lengthy historical novel or drama. He differs, however, from the Byzantine and modern Greek chronicler by striving to give the "what" and the "why" of history. The artistic sensitivity of the priest-chronicler looms large in the long passages of historical narrative in which a cultivated technique and a discipline engendered by a spiritual need to use the pen of the historian are all too evident. This inspired and inspiring work could only have been compiled and worked into a unity by a man of his background and personality. By charting a new path through the maze of literary and historical traditions, he developed his own technique.

The author, first of all, tries to convince the reader that whatever he writes is true and authentic and that he has collected the facts from old manuscripts, books, and folk traditions, and he quotes writer after writer to bring this out. Then he becomes an apologist for the people's faith in oracles, visions, and prophecies. He uses the vehicle of historical narrative to justify this faith. He launches into an attack against all those who are not true to the established moral values inherited in the race. He condemns barbarians, violators of treaties and covenants, iconoclasts, and heretics who have strayed from the established Christian ethics and dogma. Faith in Christ is a Greek faith; it is national; it represents the Greek idea and the Greek race.

The *Book of Prophecies* becomes a paean or dirge. The common chronicle in the hands of Paisius becomes a historical drama with conception, unity in the story, and stage setting. It ceases to be only a work of knowledge and becomes a creation of the imagination. Historical events are interwoven with myth. Folk legend and fairy tale emerge from historical reality, and these Paisius puts in their proper place. He becomes the storyteller. The Greek storytellers always believed that the epic poets and rhapsodes of antiquity were their immediate ancestors, and Paisius is no exception.

Had he lived in antiquity, he would have come down to us as a follower and pupil of either Homer or Herodotus, who were not only historians but theologians, not only explorers and travelers in quest of knowledge, but popular storytellers who believed in monsters, oracles, divine signs, and divine retribution. Another affinity exists with Homer and Herodotus, for all three had a passionate fondness for and pride in their native towns, and a compassion for the lot and sufferings of their fellow man. Paisius may have exploited men shamelessly on more than one occasion, but he nevertheless believed in them. Behind the narrative of Paisius, we discern the father-confessor, the Christian apologist, the patriot. On turning over the last leaf of the *Book of Prophecies,* we remain with a contented feeling that we have found something very much our own, something which we had forgotten long ago. Thanks to a handful of authors, of whom Paisius was one, a prose style was developed which enabled modern Greek literature to thrive over the years, however weakly, until it finally blossomed forth into the mature creations of the twentieth century.

Notes and References

Chapter One

1. Timothy Ware, *Eustratios Argenti* (Oxford, 1964), p. 35.
2. George Finley, *The History of Greece* (London, 1856), p. 285.
3. P. P. Argenti and S. P. Kyriakides, *Descriptions of Chios by Geographers and Travellers* (Athens, 1946), pp. 171–81.
4. George Zolotas, *History of Chios,* 3 vols. (Athens, 1923, in Greek), *passim.*
5. A. M. Vlastos, *History of Chios,* II (London, 1913, in Greek), pp. 80 and 92.
6. P. P. Argenti and S. P. Kyriakides, p. 307.
7. *Ibid.,* p. 157.
8. The word propaganda was brought into English through its use in this title.
9. F. C. Balfour, trans., *The Travels of Macarius, Patriarch of Antioch* (London, 1836), p. 342.
10. Pietro Pompilo Rodota, *Del Rito Greco in Italia* (Rome, 1758) III, Ch. 7, p. 208, and *passim.*

Chapter Two

1. C. A. Papadopoulos, *The Patriarchs of Jerusalem in the Seventeenth Century* (Jerusalem, 1907, in Greek), p. 91.
2. Vlastos, p. 80.
3. S. Lampros, *Catalogue of the Greek Manuscripts on Mt. Athos,* I (Cambridge, 1895), p. 198.
4. Rodota, p. 208.
5. A. A. Pallis, *Greek Miscellany* (Athens, 1964), p. 71.
6. W. Palmer, *The Patriarch and the Tsar,* III (London, 1873), p. 2.
7. W. Miller, *The Balkans* (London, 1899), p. 62.
8. For a good introduction to the history of Romania see N. Iorga, *History of Rumania,* trans. by J. McCabe (London, 1925).
9. W. Miller, p. 68.
10. T. E. Evangelides, *Education Under Ottoman Rule,* II (Athens, 1936), p. 355 and *passim.*

11. E. Legrand, *Bibliographie Hellénique,* IV (Paris, 1896), p. 20.
12. The MS is in the library of Lincoln College.
13. J. Mavrogordato, *Digenes Akrites* (Oxford, 1956), p. xix.
14. E. Legrand, *Bibliothèque grecque vulgaire,* II (Paris, 1881), p. 314.
15. Verses 2329–38 in Legrand.

Chapter Three

1. A. Fortesque, *The Orthodox Church* (London, 1929), p. 28.
2. T. Ware, *The Orthodox Church* (Harmondsworth, 1964, Penguin Books), p. 13.
3. For Russian sources on the relationship between Souchanov and Ligarides, and on Ligarides in general, see Cyril Mango, *The Homilies of Photius* (Cambridge, Mass., 1958), Introduction.
4. E. Legrand, *Bibliographie Hellénique,* IV (Paris, 1896), p. 21, and C. A. Papadopoulos, p. 93, citing Dositheus *On the Patriarchs of Jerusalem* (Bucharest, 1715), p. 1180.
5. G. Hoffman, *Orientalia Christiana,* XXV, 2 (1932), pp. 287, 288.
6. The letter is published by J. Sakkeliou in *Parnassus,* X (1886), pp. 482–83.
7. The confession of Faith was published by Zerlentis in *Deltion Istorikis ke Ethnologikis Eterias tis Ellados,* VI (1901), pp. 49–50.
8. Papadopoulos, p. 94, citing Lawrovsky.
9. Hoffman, p. 282.
10. In the National Library.
11. K. I. Dyovouniotes, *Nea Sion,* XVII (1922), pp. 282–87.
12. Legrand, p. 21.

Chapter Four

1. Macarius, *Travels,* p. 342.
2. Allatius in Greek means "of salt."
3. G. Zolotas, *History of Chios,* IIIA (Athens, 1923, in Greek), pp. 448, 449.
4. The Greek expression is "carrying owls to Athens."
5. Legrand, p. 55.
6. Lampros, *Catalogue,* No. 2320 (307), p. 198.
7. *Book of Prophecies,* fols. 1, 2.
8. R. W. Seton-Watson, *History of the Rumanians* (Cambridge, 1934), pp. 77, 78.
9. For details of the surrender see H. Hionides, "The Siege and Fall of Candia," *Cretica Chronica,* III (Heraclion, 1949), pp. 430–505.
10. Palmer, III, p. 7.
11. *Ibid.,* p. 586 in Nicon's *Replies.*

12. Pallis, p. 92.
13. "Travels of Macarius," pp. 342–45. The French translation is by Basile Radu. See *Patrologia Orientalis,* XXII (Paris, 1930). Russian and Romanian translations also exist.
14. "Travels of Macarius," p. 345.
15. *Ibid.,* p. 342.
16. A Book of Gospels in Greek printed in Venice in 1586 was once the property of Macarius of Antioch and found its way in the collection of John Ruskin. It is now in the Gennadius Library of Athens.
17. Palmer, III, p. 8. See also Legrand, IV, p. 24.
18. Palmer, II, xxv.

Chapter Five

1. A. P. Stanley, *Lectures on the History of the Eastern Church,* 3rd ed. (London, 1861), p. 328.
2. Lady Laura Ridding, ed., *The Travels of Macarius* (London, 1936), p. 36.
3. *Ibid.,* p. 36.
4. Stanley, p. 329.
5. Fortesque, p. 299.
6. Stanley, p. 334, quoting *The Travels of Macarius.*
7. Fortesque, p. 299.
8. Ridding, p. 118.
9. Palmer, III, viii.
10. Papadopoulos, p. 95.
11. It was so called because its sacred buildings were exact reproductions of the holy sites in Jerusalem.
12. Papadopoulos, pp. 96, 97.
13. See a detailed analysis of the Photian problem and the role of Paisius Ligarides in Cyril Mango, *Homilies.*
14. Papadopoulos, p. 97.
15. *Ibid.,* p. 98.
16. The letter has been published in its entirety by Delikanis in *Patriarchal Documents,* III (Constantinople, 1905), pp. 73–87.
17. Palmer, II, xlii.
18. Ridding, p. 118.
19. Russian nobles.
20. Palmer, II, xii.
21. Stanley, p. 341, citing Levesque.
22. Palmer, II, xiv.
23. Papadopoulos, p. 102.
24. *Ibid.,* p. 105.

25. Claudius Aelianus (fl. 200 A.D.) was the author of *De Animalium Natura* in seventeen books. These abound in hearsay and marvelous anecdotes.
26. Paisius wrote a preface to the *Nomocanon* of Matthew Blastaris which survives on Mount Athos. It is cited by Lampros, I, p. 148 and E. Eustratiades, *On the Library of Mount Athos,* I, p. 112.
27. Papadopoulos, p. 124.
28. Matthew, Chapter 23, p. 24.
29. Papadopoulos, p. 124.
30. Palmer, III, p. 9.
31. *Ibid.,* II, xv.
32. Papadopoulos, p. 125.
33. Palmer, II, xvi.
34. Legrand, IV, pp. 25–49, quoting N. Kapterev. The French translation is from the original Russian documents.
35. *Ibid.,* p. 27.
36. *Ibid.,* p. 28.
37. A liquor, mixture of honey and water.
38. Legrand, p. 29.
39. *Ibid.,* p. 30.
40. The letter was published by P. Zerlentis in the article on the "Ephimerides of John Caryophylles" in the *Deltion Istorikis ke Ethnologikis Eterias tis Ellados,* III, pp. 291–92 (in Greek).
41. *Ibid.,* p. 291.
42. Zerlentis, p. 291.
43. Papadopoulos, p. 126.
44. Palmer, II, xv.
45. An allusion to the monastery built by Nicon which he called the New Jerusalem.
46. Palmer, I, p. 46.
47. Papadopoulos, p. 128.
48. *Ibid.,* pp. 128, 129.
49. *Book of Prophecies,* fol. 216.
50. Stanley, p. 345.
51. Papadopoulos, p. 139.
52. *Ibid.,* p. 141.
53. "Parnassus," XI, pp. 462–67.
54. Palmer, II, xxvi.
55. *Ibid.*
56. *Ibid.*
57. *Ibid.,* p. xxix.
58. Published by Delikanis, *op. cit.,* pp. 119–121.
59. Papadopoulos, p. 143.
60. *Ibid.*

61. *Ibid.*
62. *Ibid.*
63. *Ibid.*, p. 146.
64. *Ibid.*, citing Macarius, *History of the Church*, XI, pp. 519–522.
65. The modern Ulyanovsk, where Lenin resided for a time. It was also the home of the Russian writer Goncharov.
66. Papadopoulos, pp. 147–148.
67. T. Vallianos, translation into Greek of Mouraviev's *History of the Russian Church* (Athens, 1851), pp. 250–251.
68. Papadopoulos, p. 150.
69. Manuscripts 469 of the Holy Synod in Moscow and 371 of the Romanian Academy.
70. Stanley, p. 346.
71. Ridding, pp. 121–122.
72. Stanley, pp. 348–349.
73. Vallianos, pp. 257–258.
74. Palmer, II, xxxvii.
75. Papadopoulos, p. 162.
76. Palmer, II, xxxvii.
77. Nectarius resigned on January 23, 1669, and the learned Dositheus was to be patriarch from 1669 to 1707.
78. Palmer, II, xxxviii.
79. *Ibid.*, p. xxxix.
80. Papadopoulos, p. 164.
81. Palmer, II, xxxix.
82. The official excommunication is published in its entirety by Papadopoulos, pp. 165–67; also in Delikanis, *Patriarchal Documents*, III (1905), pp. 188–89.
83. Papadopoulos, pp. 167, 168; "Ellenikos Filologikos Syllogos," XVII, pp. 83–85, an article by A. Papadopoulos-Kerameus.
84. Reutenfelsius.
85. Papadopoulos, p. 171.
86. *Ibid.*
87. For a detailed history of the manuscript tradition see the introduction in Mango's *Homilies of Photius*.
88. Paisius was then about sixty years of age.
89. Palmer, III, p. 8.
90. Mango, p. 15.
91. Papadopoulos, p. 168.
92. *Ibid.*, p. 169.
93. Scholars have referred to the manuscript on occasion, and a few meager excerpts from the voluminous work have been cited.
94. G. Cornoutos, *Logioi tis Turkocratias* (Athens, 1956, in the entry on Allatius).

95. Palmer, II, pp. 4, 5.
96. The other was Neophytus, metropolitan of Adrianople.
97. P. Zerlentis, *Deltion*, III, pp. 275–300.
98. British Museum MS. Additional, No. 8232.

Chapter Six

1. MS. 1327; K. Dyovouniotes, *Nea Sion*, XVII (1922), pp. 374–388.
2. Compare Curzon's description made in 1834 in his *Visits to the Monasteries of the Levant* (London, 1916), Ch. 13.
3. See article by B. Laourdas in the *Epiteris Eterias Vyzantinon Spoudon*, XXI (Athens, 1951), on the categories of letter writing established by Photius.
4. Fols. 1–17.
5. The Turks.
6. Flourished about 400 B.C. At the request of the people of Croton he painted a composite Helen from among the most beautiful maidens of that city.
7. Revered by the Russians, and perhaps of Russian (Scythian) origin. He prophesied (c. 920 A.D.) that Constantinople and the Christians would be liberated from the Turks by a "Fair Race."
8. The campaign against the Poles in 1654 was an uninterrupted success. Scores of towns including the great fortress of Smolensk fell into the hands of the Russians.
9. His reported personal meeting with Metrophanes is highly dubious.
10. Cyril III, and not Lukaris.
11. German philologist and historian (1526–1607), professor of Greek at Tübingen.
12. Legrand, *Bibliographie*, IV (Paris, 1893), p. 21.
13. *Ibid.*, p. 50.
14. The work was incorporated by Wm. Palmer in his *The Patriarch and The Tzar*, III (London, 1873).
15. Fols. 258, 259.
16. In 1644 the Knights of Malta captured three galleys laden with enormous treasure and distinguished Turks who were on a pilgrimage to Mecca.
17. *I.e.*, the Admiral of the Fleet.
18. Crete fell finally to the Turks in 1669 after a frightful war lasting twenty-five years.

Chapter Seven

1. That is, the Turks.
2. Fol. 240.

3. Fol. 232.
4. 1 and 2 Timothy, IV, 1 and III, 1.
5. N. Polites, *Paradoses tu Ellinikou Laou* (Athens, 1904), p. 1240.
6. Fols. 207–16.
7. Compare J. C. Lawson, *Modern Greek Folklore and Ancient Greek Religion* (Cambridge, 1910), p. 329.
8. Fol. 216.
9. Fols. 218–21.
10. Legendary priest and philosopher of Egypt.
11. Fols. 221–23.
12. Lawson, p. 47.

Chapter Eight

1. For authoritative studies on the complex problem of Byzantine and modern Greek oracles see N. A. Beës, *Byzantinisch-Neugriechische Jahrbücher,* XIII (Athens, 1937), 202–44 (in Greek); C. Mango, "Viz. Institut, Zbornik radova" (Belgrade, 1960), 59–93 (in English); and B. Knös, "Les Oracles de Léon le Sage" in *Aphieroma sti mnimi tu Manoli Triantafilidi* (Athens, 1960), pp. 155–188 (in French). Also A. Kominis, "Observations on the Oracles of Leo the Wise," in *E.E.B.S.,* XXX (Athens, 1960–61), 398–412 (in Greek).
2. Fols. 143–145, published by B. Laourdas in *Cretica Chronika,* II (Heraclion, 1952).
3. Beës, p. 205.
4. *Ibid.,* p. 206.
5. Fols. 170–72.
6. Beës, p. 210, fn.
7. Fol. 167.
8. Fol. 183.
9. Beës, p. 210.
10. Mango, p. 80.
11. Especially Beës and Mango.
12. Fol. 156.
13. Fol. 153.
14. Mango, p. 81.
15. Beës, p. 244.
16. Fol. 2.
17. Fols. 268–71.
18. Fol. 240.
19. Polites, *Paradoses,* I, p. 22.
20. Fols. 154, 155.
21. Polites, I, pp. 19, 20.

Chapter Nine

1. Papadopoulos-Kerameus, *Ierosolymitiki Bibliothiki,* I (1891), pp. 255–57; III (1899), pp. 327, 328.
2. There is in the Gennadius Library of Athens a Greek Book of Gospels printed in Venice in 1586 containing some manuscript notes in Arabic. On page 58 is found the signature of Macarius, patriarch of Antioch from 1647 to 1672. This Gospel was probably in his collection, and curiously enough was once owned by John Ruskin.
3. Metochion Panagiou Taphou 23 of Constantinople, Papadopoulos-Kerameus, *Iero. Bibl.,* IV (1899), p. 36.
4. Fols. 246 and 260.
5. Fol. 243. Innocent died in January, 1655.
6. *Byzantinische Zeitschrift,* XII (1903), pp. 268–72.
7. B. Laourdas, *Cretica Chronica,* II (1952).
8. E. Legrand, *Bibliographie Hellénique,* III (1841), p. 67.
9. C. Mango, *Viz. Institut, Zbornik radova, passim.*
10. Matthew flourished at the turn of the seventeenth century.
11. Fols. 113–30.
12. Flourished in the fifteenth century, both before and after the fall.
13. Fol. 191.
14. Fol. 192.
15. Fol. 240.
16. Fols. 136, 137.
17. Fol. 139.
18. Fol. 166.
19. Fol. 148.
20. Fol. 182.
21. Fol. 82, the twenty-fourth oracle.
22. Fol. 79.
23. Fol. 160.
24. Fol. 168.
25. Fol. 179.
26. Fol. 134.
27. *Ibid.*
28. Fol. 143.
29. Fols. 156 sq., and fols. 264 sq.
30. Mango. pp. 87–88.
31. Quoted from L. Magnus, *A Dictionary of European Literature,* 2nd ed. (London, 1927), in the entry on Chateaubriand, p. 93.

Chapter Ten

1. See R. M. Dawkins, "Graeco-Barbara," from a paper read at Oxford on May 28, 1938 before the Philological Society.
2. Fol. 156.

Selected Bibliography

(The bibliography does not include the numerous secondary sources that refer to Paisius Ligarides in passing; nor does it include the historical works that cover the period. Most sources for Paisius are to be found in Moscow. Fortunately, some of these are available in English and other translations. The book has been based for the most part on the hitherto unpublished manuscripts of Paisius.)

PRIMARY SOURCES

ALLATIUS, L. *De Ecclesiae Occidentalis atque Orientalis Perpetua Consensione*, III. Cologne, 1648.

AMANTOS, C. "Paisius Ligarides" in the *Annual of Byzantine Studies of Athens*, XIII. Athens, 1937 (in Greek).

ARCADIUS, P. *Peri tu Katharteriou Pyros kata Varlaam.* Rome, 1637 (in Greek and Latin).

DELIKANIS, K. *Patriarchal Documents*, III. Constantinople, 1905 (in Greek).

DOSITHEOS (PATRIARCH). *History of the Patriarchs of Jerusalem.* Bucharest, 1715 (in Greek).

DYOVOUNIOTIS, C. Unpublished Sermons of P. Ligarides in *Nea Sion*, XVII. 1922 (in Greek).

ERNSTEDT, V. E., A. KUNIK, and P. NIKITAN. *Mémoires de l'Académie impériale des sciences*, VII (8). St. Petersburg, 1906 (in Russian).

GRUMEL, V. "Paisius Ligarides" in *Dictionnaire de Théologie Catholique*, IX. Paris, 1926.

HOFFMAN, G. "Patriarchen von Konstantinopel," *Orientalia Christiana*, XXV and XXXII. Rome, 1932 and 1933.

JOACHIM, IVIRITES. "Praxis heirotonias Paisiou Ligaridou" in *Gregory Palamas*, X. Athens, 1917 (in Greek).

LAMBROS, S. *Catalogue of the Greek Codices of Mt. Athos.* Cambridge, I, 1895.

LAOURDAS, B. "Paisius Ligarides and the Cretan Oracles," in *Cretica Chronica.* Heraclion, II, 1952 (in Greek).

———. "Paisius Ligarides and Photius" in *Orthodoxia*, XXVI, Constantinople, 1951 (in Greek).

LAVROSKY, L. Details on the biography of P. Ligarides in the *Journal de l'Académie*. St. Petersburg, 1889 (in Russian).
LEGRAND, E. *Bibliographie Hellénique*, IV. Paris, 1896.
MANGO, C. "The Legend of Leo the Wise" in *Viz. Institut Zbornik radova*, VI. Belgrade, 1960 (in English).
———. *The Homilies of Photius*. Harvard, 1958.
PALMER, W. *The Patriarch and the Tsar*. London, 1871–76, especially Volume III, 1873 (from which I have taken the translations of Russian sources).
PAPADOPOULOS, C. A. *The Patriarchs of Jerusalem as Spiritual Leaders of Russia in the 17th Century*. Jerusalem, 1907 (in Greek).
———. "Peri tis Praxeos tis heirotonias tu Paisiou Ligaridou os Metropolitou Gazis," in *Gregory Palamas*, X. 1917 (in Greek).
———. Letter of P. Ligarides in *Ecclesiastiki Alethia*, XXV. 1905 (in Greek).
PAUL OF ALEPPO. *The Travels of Macarius*, translated from the Arabic by F. C. Balfour. London, 1834.
RODOTA, P. P. *Del Rito Greco in Italia*. Rome, 1758.
SAKELLION, J. and A. "Letter of Paisius" in *Parnassos*, X. 1886 (in Greek).
———. *Catalogue of MSS in the National Library of Greece*. Athens, 1892.
SALOMAN, R. "Paisius Ligarides," *Zeitschrift für Osteuropäische Geschichte*, V, 1931.
SATHAS, C. *Neoelliniki Philologia*. Athens, 1868.
VLASTOS, A. M. *Chiaka*. Hermoupolis, 1840 (in Greek).
ZAVIRAS, G. I. "Paisius Ligarides" in *Nea Hellas*. Athens, 1872 (in Greek).
ZERLENTIS, P. "Paisius Ligarides, Confession of Faith," in *Deltion tis istorikis ke ethnologikis eterias tis Ellados*, VI. Athens, 1901 (in Greek).
ZOLOTAS, G. I. *History of Chios*. Athens, 1923 (in Greek).

SECONDARY SOURCES

BEËS, N. "On the related oracle . . . ," in *Byzantinisch-Neugriechische Jahrbücher* (2–4). Athens, 1937 (in Greek).
DEMETRACOPOULOS, A. *Orthodox Greece*. Leipzig, 1872 (in Greek).
EFSTRATIADES, S. *Libraries of Mt. Athos*, I. Paris, 1925.
EVANGELIDES, T. E. *Education under Ottoman Rule*, II. Athens, 1936 (in Greek).
GEDEON, M. *Patriarchiki Pinakes*. Constantinople, 1886 (in Greek).
KAPTEREV, N. *Character of Relationships between Russia and the Orthodox East in the 16th and 17th Centuries*. Moscow, 1885 (in Russian).

———. *The Patriarch Nicon and Tsar Alexis.* Moscow, 1902–12 (in Russian).

LITZICA, C. *Biblioteca Academiei Romane, Catalogul manuscriptelor grecesti.* Bucharest, 1909.

MOURAVIEFF, A. N. *History of the Russian Church* (English translation by Blackmore). London, 1842.

PALEOLOGOS, C. "Relationships between the Church of Jerusalem and Russia," in *Parnassos*, XI. Athens, 1888 (in Greek).

PAPADOPOULOS-KERAMEUS, A. *Ierosolymitiki Vivliothiki,* I, III. St. Petersburg, 1891 (in Greek).

VALLIANOS, T. *History of the Russian Church* (a Greek translation of the Russian). Athens, 1851.

VAPHIDES, PH. *History of the Church, III.* Constantinople, 1912 (in Greek).

Index

(The works of Paisius Ligarides are listed under his name)